1,000 favorite quotes

1,000 favorite quotes
Much Wisdom in short sayings

Written and compiled by Victor Arias Jr.

To my Aunt Ofelia,

Who has always enjoyed my narratives, and to all who enjoy good quotes and wisdom.

Acknowledgments

I want to thank God first and foremost and above all, for giving me the inspiration, the time and the guidance to develop and complete this work. To my parents Victor Arias; and Dinorah Nina; for their support and for bringing me up, directing me on the way I should go. To Gerson; my brother and Germaly; my sister for embracing the project.

As well as my uncle Samuel Nina Ortiz; for his great ideas and assistance. To my cousin Carlos Nina Jr. for his tips and cooperation.

To my friend Dave Fiedler; for his continuous collaboration; and to my friends: Walter Saravia; Rodolfo Baez; and to all whom, in some way, made possible the execution and success of this work.

Table of Contents

Foreword

The wisest man who ever lived once counseled us that "Wisdom is the principal thing; therefore get wisdom."[1] In fact, he wrote a whole book on the topic, trying to boil this ideal of wisdom down into the words and images of everyday life. And today, thousands of years later, wisdom is still the main thing in life. What's more, it's often still best captured in those well-chosen words which strike to the heart of a subject, and lock the idea in the mind.

Who hasn't found themselves caught tongue-tied at just the wrong moment, but knowing that there was the perfect idea... out there... somewhere? That's when we usually realize the value of wisdom! Even more importantly, however, are those moments when a decision is pressing to be made. What to do? Which way to turn? What principles of life to build on? That's when we need wisdom the most!

Unfortunately, our culture has largely turned away from the thoughtful, organized kind of wisdom that was a staple of practical education in years past. Today, we're more likely to make a decision based on the plot of a sit-com or a movie. This isn't always bad; even entertainment can embody wisdom... it's just that so little of it does. After all, wisdom would probably argue against purchasing about 99% of what shows up in the commercials.

So here's an alternative: why not make wisdom "the principal thing," and recognize that even in serious issues there are entertaining gems that make us laugh... and think.

The volume you hold in your hand has been some time in the making. I've had the privilege of watching the process of compilation from a distance. (Like most people, I enjoy watching someone else do the hard work on a project that holds out promise

---

1 Proverbs 4:7
   King James Version (KJV)

of value.) This, too, has been entertaining. Never hilarious, occasionally humorous, but primarily entertaining. It has been a show worth watching. And now that the months of collection, categorization, and arrangement are finished, I believe you will find both wisdom and entertainment in its pages. And with this, I believe you will be benefited and the compiler will be pleased.

—Dave Fiedler

Introduction

It was in 2010 when I became interested in reading good quotes. In the fall of that year I decided to create a page in social media where I could have them in one place and share them with friends.

I would post one or two quotes every day. I liked doing this and I was learning from it. One night I came across a quote I really liked, for it described what I was doing and made me realize it:

"The smallest of disciplines, practiced every day, start an incredible process that can change our lives forever."[1]

I continued doing it for two years and decided to pick and save one thousand favorite quotes. I thought of that amount for no specific reason other than it was a good number based on the amount that so far I had enjoyed reading and sharing. It was during 2012, after having collected almost one thousand favorite quotes that I had the idea to put them in an actual book. This way more people could read them and be blessed.

The book was going to be permanent. Who knows what was going to happen to social media or its posts or its policies? The book could be read offline. You could leave it on the table. You could read it on planes, in bathtubs, in church.

I shared the idea to friends and they found it attractive and liked it. While working on this book, I read another quotation that caught my attention. It helped me see how good of a decision it had been.

"When we once begin to form good resolutions, God gives us every opportunity of carrying them out."

---

[1] The quotes mentioned above and their authors can be found in this book with its index of authors.

I saw that God was opening doors. I had the support and the necessary tools to start the project, plus everyone liked the plan.

I had picked one thousand favorite random quotes but they were all random. One quotation for instance would talk about "Goals," the next about "Worship," and the next about "Criticism," so for the book I thought it was going to be nice to organize and divide them into topics. I shared the decision with friends and they found the categorizing idea great for referencing sake.

So first, I needed to identify the main subject of each quote; usually it could be easily identified by the key word of the sentence. For instance, 11 different ones would talk about the "Mind" then 9 different ones would talk about "Decision" and 4 different ones would talk about "Creativity" and so forth.

Now that I had the main subjects of the quotes identified, the title name for the topics would be named after the same word the sentence was talking about—the "Mind" for instance—thus creating a well referenced stack of quotes by topics. And while discovering different related topics, I would group these together and separate those from others with quotes about a different subject: "Adversity," "Problems," "Worry," "Difficulty," "Trial," "Struggle," etc.

Now I had several related topics, referenced on their quotes. I needed a chapter name that would suggest the content of all the related topics for that chapter... and while building new chapters all from one thousand random quotes, it's amazing how well connected all the quotes and the different chapters ended up. I was always surprised to see how well they were falling in place. One of my favorite chapters where you see this happening is "The Son of God" with beautiful quotations in concatenation, packed with meaningful descriptions about Jesus, His Birth, His Ministry, His Crucifixion and His Resurrection and the relationship we need with Him.

It was challenging work, connecting or linking in series one thousand favorite random quotes, and arranging chapters following the best possible pattern tailored to address the steps to a life of success.

It was a lot of fun, but it was also a lot of work, and sometimes I would ask to myself why I had to pick one thousand quotes for the book... and just at the right time, I read two quotes I needed:

"Don't give up on what God has called you to do; the end result is worth the pain."

"Don't give up on the things God has placed in your heart. Keep pushing and praying He will direct you."

These words gave me the boost needed to keep at it, and I felt impelled to work until the end—especially after reading this quote dead on target:

"We are a culture that relies on technology over community, a society in which spoken and written words are cheap, easy to come by, and excessive. Our culture says anything goes; fear of God is almost unheard of. We are slow to listen, quick to speak, and quick to become angry."

The message of this book is to help reverse the bad course of our culture. Where we would rely on community over technology, where the spoken and written words of our society would not be cheap and easy to come by, and excessive but of value, a culture that would not promote "you can do anything you want and forget about the consequences," and that would understand the fear of the Lord. That we would learn to listen and to surrender our impulses before becoming angry and speaking.

"There are many ways to live your life, but it is your calling to choose the right one."

These one thousand favorite quotes are a great aid to a life of success: with Jesus by our side on the steps we choose to take.

This grand compendium with over one hundred important topics distributed in twenty remarkable chapters, will teach you about approaching everyday life situations differently. You will learn about leadership, finance, health, relationships, and more about Jesus from a "quotes perspective" and the life eternal He longs to give us. Quotes which have been thought of from those who experienced God working in their lives sharing and living what Christianity is all about. Other authors, though they may not identify themselves with a religion in particular, what they said is remarkable, worthy of notice, important in effect and meaning. This unique compilation provides words of counsel and inspiration wherever you may be right this second.

At the end of some chapters, the reader will also encounter fun sections with humorous quotations and or an artful play on words, a break for laughter between chapters. I hope you find this compendium to be a valuable resource in your study library for years to come, for a good quote never gets old.

"Some books are to be tasted, others to be swallowed, and some few to be chewed and digested."[2] ...including this one.

—Victor Arias Jr.

---

[2] Sir Francis Bacon. English author, courtier, & philosopher (1561 - 1626).

Chapter One

Living

-----◆◆◆-----

Life:

"One thing I've learned from life is that Life Is A Sum Of
All Your Choices; Choose Wisely and Make Good Ones."   1

"There are several ways to live your life. But it's your
call to choose the Right one."   2

"The meaning of life is to find your gift. The purpose of
life is to give it away."   3

"We make a living by what we get; we make a life by
what we give."   4

"It's the donation, not the duration of your life that matters. Not how long you live, but how well you live."   5

"I trust God with my life; after all, He gave it to me."   6

"Life is God's novel. Let Him write it."   7

"The point of your life is to point to Him. Whatever you are doing, God wants to be glorified, because this whole thing is His."   8

"You were made by God and for God. Until you understand that, life will never make sense."   9

"There are two great days in a person's life—the day we are born and the day we discover why."   10

"Life is not a progression of fixed points. In fact, stable times actually are the exception; transition is the norm."   11

"Your life isn't a status update in social media."   12

"Life is more than a game; it's a journey with eternal implications. Don't spend it in trivial pursuits."   13

"Our calling is to live in our bodies now in a way which anticipates the life we shall live then."   14

"Life is preparation for eternity. It's the practice for the main event."   15

"Life is like a piano. It has bright days and dark ones. But if you know how to play, it makes a beautiful song."   16

"With every rising of the sun, think of your life as just begun."   17

"Never let a bad day make you feel like you will have a bad life."   18

"Work for a cause, not for applause. Live life to express, not to impress. Don't strive to make your presence noticed just make your absence felt."
19

"Look at life through the windshield, not the rear view mirror."
20

"If you are not hearing from God, it might not be because He is silent; it might be because your life is too noisy."
21

"One of the signs God's working in your life is He's bringing difficult people into your life, for you to love them."
22

"Alone, hearts are one of life's most fragile things, but together their passion can accomplish the impossible."
23

"The major value in life is not what you get. The major value in life is what you become. That is why I wish to pay fair price for every value. If I have to pay for it or earn it, that makes something of me. If I get it for free, that makes nothing of me."
24

"The great lie so many of us chase is the illusion that anything created can give life ultimate meaning."   25

"The greatest pleasure in life is doing what people say you cannot do."   26

"Life's greatest losses prepare us for our greatest victories."   27

"The measure of a life, after all, is not its duration, but its donation."   28

"Life is not measured by the number of breaths we take but by the moments that take our breath away."   29

"There are only two ways to live your life. One is as though nothing is a miracle. The other is as if everything is."   30

"Since I know God loves me totally and wants what's best for me, I don't have to understand every move He makes in my life."   31

"God is not just asking what you are willing to die for, but what are you willing to live for."

32

"God can use an ordinary life to bring extraordinary blessings into the world."

33

"Old age isn't the winter of life, it is the harvest."

34

"And in the end, it's not the years in your life that count. It's the life in your years."

35

"It doesn't matter what we have or what we accomplish in life. In the end what truly matters is who we have beside us."

36

"In the long run, we shape our lives, and we shape ourselves. The process never ends until we die. And the choices we make are ultimately our own responsibility."

37

"Every action in our lives touches on some chord that will vibrate in eternity."

38

"Works done in God's name long outlive our earthly
lives."   39

"Here is the test to find whether your mission on earth
is finished. If you're alive, it isn't."   40

"Enjoy the little things in life, for one day you may look
back and realize they were the big things."   41

"We are in for a sad life if we let other people
determine our level of joy."   42

"Many times we get discouraged not because life is
hard, but because we take problems too seriously."   43

"The trick is to enjoy life. Don't wish away your days,
waiting for better ones ahead."   44

"Some of the best days of your life are still ahead of
you."   45

Eutrapelia I

"Laughter and joy shouldn't be guests in your house; they should be permanent residents in your everyday life."

"A smile is the lighting system of the face, the cooling system of the head and the heating system of the heart."

"We are all here for a spell; get all the good laughs you can."

"There are three types of people in the world: those who can count & those who can't."

Definition of Eutrapelia: see page 281

Chapter Two

Noetic

———◆◆◆———

Noetic - Pertaining to, or originating in the mind

Mind:

"Before you were born to your parents, you were born in the mind of God."

1

"The tough mind is sharp and penetrating, breaking through the crust of legends and myths and sifting the true from the false."

2

"Nourish the mind like you would your body. The mind cannot survive on junk food."

3

"Always give a piece of your heart, not a piece of your mind."

4

"Your thoughts become your words and your attitude. Where the mind goes, the man follows."

5

"Keep your mind going in the right direction, and your life will catch up with it."

6

"Don't let negative pictures play on the movie screen of your mind. You own the remote control. All you have to do is change the channel."

7

"The leg does not feel the chains when the mind is in the heavens."

8

"You have to get your mind going in a new direction, because dwelling on negative thoughts will keep you from becoming all God has created you to be."

9

"Knowing about Jesus is not the same thing as knowing Jesus. An informed mind is not the same thing as an inflamed heart."

10

"If you want to have the mind of Christ, you must see yourself as His servant on earth."   11

Decision:

"Every day requires a decision to be a living sacrifice because we all have a tendency to slide off the altar."   1

"Everyone is always just one decision away from a disaster. Ask for wisdom!" James 1:5-6   2

"Make decisions based on what you know rather than what you feel."   3

"Don't mourn over your bad decisions, just start overcoming them with good ones."   4

"Our future is not tied to making the right decisions but trusting the right Lord."   5

"The only person you are destined to become is the person you decide to be."   6

"The possibilities are numerous once we decide to act and not react."

7

"Indecision is debilitating; it feeds upon itself; it is, one might almost say, habit-forming. Not only that, but it is contagious; it transmits itself to others."

8

"Indecision is the thief of opportunity."

9

Choice:

"We should choose the right because it is right, and leave consequences with God."

1

"Don't choose career over ministry."

2

"Don't choose ministry over family."

3

"Growing older is automatic. Growing up is a choice."

4

"We, like David, have two choices: flee or face the giant."   5

"Abraham gave Lot the choice of where he would go so that afterward Lot should not be tempted to think that in the separation Abraham had his own interest in view. Lot chose a beautiful location near Sodom. The land of his choice possessed every natural advantage, but he failed to investigate the morals and religion of the Sodomites. We have on record his after-history."   6

"I am not what has happened to me. I am what I choose to become."   7

"When tragedy strikes we're left to choose what we see. We can see either hurt or the Healer."   8

"You may choose to look the other way but you can never say again that you did not know."   9

Maturity:

"Age is no guarantee of maturity."   1

"Maturity is putting up with those you could easily put down."

2

"Losses may deepen me, but they don't define me. They're part of maturity, but not my identity."

3

Creativity:

"The greatest enemy of creativity is 'We've always done it that way.'"

1

"Creativity is allowing yourself to make mistakes. Art is knowing which ones to keep."

2

"Creativity is natural. Discipline is not. But you need discipline to amplify creativity."

3

"A creative man is motivated by the desire to achieve, not by the desire to beat others."

4

Freedom:

"The purpose of freedom is to create it for others."

1

"We must have the freedom to dream, the courage to risk, the faith to believe, and the will to succeed."   2

Liberty:

"Liberty means responsibility. That is why most men dread it."   1

"Stand fast therefore in the liberty wherewith Christ hath made us free, and be not entangled again with the yoke of bondage."   2

Ignorance:

"If you think education is expensive, try ignorance."   1

"The trouble with ignorance is that it picks up confidence as it goes along."   2

Judgment:

"Good judgment comes from experience, and a lot of that comes from bad judgment."   1

"Don't judge each day by the harvest you reap but by the seeds that you plant."   2

"Don't judge others. God likes variety and we've all got our own little brand of "strangeness."   3

"By judging others we blind ourselves to our own evil and to the grace which others are just as entitled to as we are."   4

"You can easily judge the character of a man [person] by how he treats those who can do nothing for him."   5

Eutrapelia II

"It's easy to spot people who can't count to ten. They're in front of you in the supermarket express lane."

"Hey, to whoever invented the zero: Thanks for nothing."

"Every man reaps what he sows, except the amateur gardener."

"I just poured superglue into a non-stick pan. Somebody is going to be wrong."

Chapter Three

Hardship

————◆◆◆————

Adversity:

"Adversity causes some men to break, and others to break records." [1]

"Sometimes our adversity is another's opportunity to encounter Christ. Persecution in Jerusalem led to the Gospel being preached in Samaria." (Acts-8) [2]

Problem:

"People everywhere offer solutions for the world's problems, but mostly they don't understand what the problem truly is." [1]

"Most problems in life have one of two causes: We act without thinking or we think without acting."   2

"Often times the mirror is a great place to look for solutions to existing problems."   3

"Objects of fear are smaller than they appear. Focusing on God, puts problems in an accurate perspective."   4

"If God knows the number of hairs on your head, what makes you think He's unaware of big problems in your life?"   5

"When you read the newspaper, you hear the poor are the problem; when you read the Bible, you hear the rich are the problem."   6

"Let God's promises shine on your problems."   7

"The problem in front of me is never as significant as the Power behind me."   8

"Too often we spend all our time seeking God for answers to our problems when what we should be doing is just seeking God."   9

"If you are always talking about your problems, don't be surprised if you live in perpetual defeat."   10

"If you want to get over a problem, stop talking about it. Your mind affects your mouth, and your mouth affects your mind."   11

"The God of your day is greater than the problems of your day. Trust Him."   12

"You must stop talking about the problem and start talking about the solution. Start speaking words of victory!"   13

Worry:

"Worry is a cycle of inefficient thoughts whirling around a center of fear."   1

"Don't worry about anyone who talks about you behind your back. They're behind you for a reason."   2

"Worry is the darkroom where negatives are developed."   3

"Worry gives small problems big shadows."   4

"Worry is a down payment on a problem you may never have."   5

"Statistics say that 10% of all people won't like us, so let's enjoy the 90% who do and stop worrying about the 10% who don't."   6

"Worry is worthless. It can't change the past. It can't control the future. It only wastes this moment."   7

"You can tell the size of your God by looking at the size of your worry list. The longer your list, the smaller your God."   8

"Worrying is wasting energy on the things you can't control. Leave everything in God's hand. Think less, pray more."   9

"Definition of anxiety: half of the time you're worried about the other half of the time."   10

"Don't worry! The Good Shepherd's ability to fix things is greater than your ability to mess things up."   11

"Don't toss and turn and worry and be anxious. Don't waste your time counting sheep. Be the sheep who runs to the Shepherd."   12

Difficulty:

"Serving God doesn't mean we'll no longer have difficulties. We're still on the battlefield, but we don't have to fight alone."   1

"Instead of dwelling on your difficulties, focus more on the fact that God is for you and His power is at work in you."   2

"No one makes a lock without a key. That's why God won't give us difficulties without a solution."   3

"When we allow God to be exalted in our difficulties, we are in the perfect place to smell the fragrance of His Presence."   4

Trial:

"God allows trials in our lives because we have a strong core of inner pride and self-sufficiency that works to our long-term detriment."   1

"We are always in the forge, or on the anvil; by trials God is shaping us for higher things."   2

Trial – Miscellaneous:

"When everything seems to be going against you, remember that the airplane takes off against the wind, not with it."   3

"Storms make oaks take deeper root."   4

Struggle:

"God-given struggles don't come to stay, they come to pass. Just be patient. Wait while God works for you."   1

"God hears and He sees, and you are not alone in your struggles. Remain firm and stable, for God has your deliverance planned."   2

Suffering:

"Like it or not, suffering is part of the package. We share in the sufferings of Christ."   1

"The greatest good that suffering can do for me is to increase my capacity for God."   2

"Just as the sufferings of Christ flow over into our lives, so also through Christ, our comfort overflows."   3

Failure:

"Failure is the condiment that gives success its flavor."   1

"Failure is not falling short of your pursuit of a great aim; it is succeeding at something that doesn't matter."   2

"Failure doesn't mean you are a failure; it just means you haven't succeeded yet."   3

"Failure is simply the opportunity to begin again, this time more intelligently."   4

"I would rather attempt something great and fail, than attempt to do nothing and succeed."   5

"Success at the expense of faith and family is really failure."   6

"It's no shame to have only one talent. The shame is in failing to develop it to the max." See Matt.25:1   7

Eutrapelia III

"Not only is my short-term memory terrible, but so is my short-term memory."

"Researchers have discovered that people will believe anything that you tell them researchers have discovered."

"Your mind needs exercise just as much as your body does. That's why I think of exercising every day."

"I used to be indecisive; now I'm not sure."

Chapter Four

Endurance

———◆◆◆———

Opportunity:

"God is placing great opportunities in your life... pause and appreciate them."   1

"It still holds true that man is most uniquely human when he turns obstacles into opportunities."   2

"Opportunity follows struggle. It follows effort. It follows hard work."   3

"When we once begin to form good resolutions, God gives us every opportunity of carrying them out."   4

Will:

"Stop saying, 'I wish' and start saying, 'I will.'"   1

"Most people have the will to win, few have the will to prepare to win."   2

"If you are not willing to risk the unusual, you will have to settle for the ordinary."   3

"Without free will, man wouldn't be made in God's image. But with it, he can defy God and bring misery on himself and others."   4

"It isn't a matter of whether you can or can't. It's whether you will or won't."   5

"You can have anything you want if you are willing to give up the belief that you can't have it."   6

"Be willing to listen to others and be teachable. You're not right about everything. Nobody is."   7

"God's will for you is not a road map; it is a relationship."   8

"We define greatness by being worthy to be served. God defines greatness by our willingness to serve the unworthy."   9

"Winners of souls must first be weepers for souls. You cannot push anyone up the ladder unless he is willing to climb."   10

"There are only two kinds of people in the end: those who say to God, 'Thy will be done,' and those to whom God says, in the end, 'Thy will be done.'"   11

Confidence:

"If your confidence comes from the praise of men, you'll be devastated by their criticisms."   1

"When we are truly confident and secure, the opinions of others cannot control us."   2

"One important key to success is self-confidence. An important key to self-confidence is preparation."   3

Confidence – Miscellaneous:

"When we can't piece together the puzzle of our own lives, remember the best view of a puzzle is from above. Let Him help put you together."   4

Goal:

"A goal without a plan is just a wish."   1

"Goals are the fuel in the furnace of achievement."   2

"The goal isn't to be better than others, but to be better than you were yesterday."   3

"God's ultimate goal for your life on earth is not comfort, but character development."   4

"If you go to work on your goals, your goals will go to work on you. If you go to work on your plan, your plan will go to work on you. Whatever good things we build up end up building us."   5

"The Apostle Paul's main goal wasn't to win converts or build churches. It was to know Jesus."   6

"Our goal in life must be an absolute surrender to God's holy will."   7

"Goals are like the stars—they are always there. Adversity is like the clouds, it is temporary and will move on. Keep your eyes on the stars."   8

Goal – Miscellaneous:

"Pilgrims and drifters are both on a journey, but pilgrims know where they're going. I'm a pilgrim not a drifter."   9

"Do not go where the path may lead, go instead where there is no path and leave a trail."   10

Plan:

"When you try to figure out everything, you're exalting your reasoning above God's thoughts and plans for your life."   1

"The number one barrier to God's Plan for your life is your plan."   2

"God's plan for your life is greater than your plan for your life."   3

Perseverance:

"Perseverance is a great element of success. If you only knock long enough at the gate, you are sure to wake up somebody."   1

"The ability to wait and persevere is so rare. No wonder God values it so highly."   2

Perseverance – Miscellaneous:

"Don't give up what you want most for what you want now."   3

"Trying times are not the times to stop trying." 4

"You can have anything you want if you want it desperately enough. You must want it with an exuberance that erupts through the skin and joins the 'energy' that created the world." 5

"All work and no play, will make you a manager." 6

"Work will win when wishing won't." 7

"Winning takes talent, to repeat takes character." 8

"I'm not telling you it is going to be easy, I'm telling you it's going to be worth it." 9

"When you know the right thing to do, there is almost always some kind of opposition. Never give up." 10

"God values persistence and obedience more than position or performance." 11

"If a bird is flying for pleasure, it flies with the wind; but if it meets danger, it turns and faces the wind in order that it may fly higher."

12

"Aerodynamically, the bumble bee shouldn't be able to fly, but the bumble bee doesn't know it so it goes on flying anyway."

13

"The difference in winning and losing is most often, not quitting."

14

"Make up your mind that you're not going to quit until you see the fruit of what God has placed within you."

15

"Run like every lap is your last. One day you'll be right."   16

"The way I see it, if you want the rainbow, you gotta put up with the rain."

17

"Things may come to those who wait, but only the things left by those who hustle."

18

"It's hard to beat a person who never gives up."   19

"Your cross comes before your crown."   20

"Don't give up on what God has called you to do. The end result is worth the pain."   21

"Don't give up on the things God has placed in your heart. Keep pushing and praying He will direct you."   22

"Walk boldly through the doors God opens for you, and don't become discouraged when He closes one."   23

Luck:

"I'm a great believer in luck and I find the harder I work, the more I have of it."   1

"Remember that not getting what you want is sometimes a wonderful stroke of luck."   2

Discipline:

"The smallest of disciplines, practiced every day, start an incredible process that can change our lives forever."   1

"Discipline is the bridge between goals and accomplishment."   2

Success:

"Success is the sum of small efforts, repeated day in and day out."   1

"The only place where success comes before work is the dictionary."   2

"Success is not counted by how high you have climbed but by how many people you brought with you."   3

"Any success I've seen has come by obeying God's instruction, trusting His promises, waiting on His timing, then risking failure."   4

"Successful people know the difference between patience and procrastination. Bitterness wastes energy that you can't afford to waste."   5

"It is not your business to succeed, but to do right; when you have done so, the rest lies with God."   6

"You don't need a mentor. You need several! No single person can teach all you need to know to succeed."   7

Achievement:

"Nothing great was ever achieved without enthusiasm."   1

"Make the most of yourself by fanning the tiny, inner sparks of possibility into flames of achievement."   2

Focus:

"The secret of change is to focus all of your energy not on fighting the old, but on building the new."   1

"Whenever you focus on what's not important, you tend to miss what is."

2

"When you focus on what's beyond your control, you miss what isn't."

3

"We cannot direct the wind, but we can adjust the sails."

4

Eutrapelia IV

"All my friends keep telling me to never succumb to peer pressure. So I'm going to take their advice and not listen to them."

"If you fall and break both of your legs, don't come running to me."

"I tried paying my bills with a smile. They wanted money."

"'Always leave them wanting more' is my standard approach to paying bills."

Chapter Five

Leading

—◆—

Lead:

"If you don't love people, you will never lead them." 1

"If you think you're leading and no one is following, you're just taking a walk!" 2

"Leaders create more leaders. Wannabes only create followers." 3

"Leaders think and talk about the solutions. Followers think and talk about the problems." 4

"Leadership is an action, not a position."   5

"Leadership means having a boat parked in your front yard for 100 years and everyone thinking you're nuts."   6

"The best leaders are reflectors of praise, not absorbers."   7

"Leaders bring out the best in others."   8

"It's wise to follow a leader whose definition of succeeding is seeing you succeed."   9

"Managers hold on, leaders let go."   10

"Leaders provide the sky that others may soar."   11

"Your role as a church leader is not to do all the ministry, but to train God's people to do ministry."   12

"The path where God leads the way may lie through the desert or the sea, but it is a safe path." 13

Lead - Miscellaneous:

"Big jobs usually go to the men who prove their ability to outgrow small ones." 14

Vision:

"Passionate hearts committed to a shared vision can accomplish the impossible." 1

"The most pathetic person in the world is someone who has sight, but has no vision." 2

"Vision is the gift to see what others only dream." 3

"I may lose my sight one day, but I don't intend to ever lose my vision." 4

Integrity:

"Integrity is a choice. It is consistently choosing the purity of truth over popularity."   1

"Integrity knows the difference between fatigue and laziness."   2

Mediocrity:

"Mediocrity will always try to drag excellence down to its level."   1

"I know of nothing more effective in inspiring excellence than to observe mediocrity."   2

"As long as you're in command, you'll be mediocre. having the means of grace at your disposal, but still getting nowhere."   3

Mediocrity – Miscellaneous:

"Our temptation is to look eagerly for the minimum that will be accepted."   4

"We live in an art gallery of divine creativity and yet we are content to gaze only at the carpet."   5

"One can never consent to creep when one feels as an impulse to soar."   6

"The danger for most of us lies not in setting our aim too high and falling short; but in setting our aim too low and achieving our mark."   7

Pride:

"The more pride we have, the more other people's pride irritates us."   1

"Don't allow your pride or personal preference to limit who you will learn from."   2

"A proud man is always looking down on things and people; and, of course, as long as you are looking down, you cannot see something that is above you."   3

"Never compare! If you think you're better than someone, you get prideful. But if you think they're better, you get discouraged."   4

Pride - Miscellaneous:

"Always hold your head up, but be careful to keep your nose at a friendly level."   5

"If you only learn from voices you agree with, your perspective will be small, your life will be shallow, and your ministry stunted."   6

"By craving to be more, man becomes less; and by aspiring to be self-satisfying, he fell away from Him who truly satisfies"   7

"None are so empty as those who are full of themselves."   8

Fool:

"Any fool can criticize, condemn, and complain - and most fools do."   1

"Wise and foolish both make mistakes. The wise learn
from them. The foolish repeat them."

2

"Better to remain silent and be thought a fool than to
speak and remove all doubt."

3

Pessimist, Optimist:

"I'm a pessimistic optimist. I expect the worst—that
way things can only get better."

1

"A stumbling block to the pessimist is a stepping stone
to the optimist."

2

"An optimist stays up until midnight to see the New
Year in. A pessimist stays up to make sure the old year
leaves."

3

Eutrapelia V

"The days of good grammar has went."

"Do you enjoy wasting time on the internet? Take this 1,500 question online quiz to find out."

"Paul was so fast that he could turn off a light and then jump into his bed before the room got dark."

"My local grocery store uses four checkouts; unless it's really busy—then they use one."

Chapter Six

Elocution

————◆◆◆————

Word:

"Never use a big word where a diminutive one will do." [1]

"Judge your worth and value by what God says about you in His Word, not by how somebody else treats you." (Ephesians 2:4-10) [2]

"Whenever the words of heaven are filtered through mortal minds, tongues, and vocabularies, there is some diminution." [3]

"Words can be used to complain or to change something. Your choice." [4]

"Whoever said, 'Sticks and stone may hurt me', but words will never harm me," was either in denial, lying or worse."   5

"Always and never are two words you should always remember never to use."   6

"If someone you know is grieving, don't try to 'fix it' with just the right words. Simply offer silent support by your presence and prayers."   7

"Words are like seeds. They have creative power. Isaiah says, 'We will eat the fruit of our words.' What seeds are you planting?"   8

"A woman has the last word in any argument. Anything a man says after that is the beginning of a new argument."   9

Say:

"If you say it offensively, it will be received defensively."   1

"What is powerful is when what you say is just the tip of the iceberg of what you know."   2

"When you have nothing to say, say nothing."   3

Say - Miscellaneous:

"You're never persuasive when you're abrasive."   4

"The phrase, 'Don't take this the wrong way' has a zero percent success rate."   5

"Fact.. If you start a sentence off, with 'no offense, but..' it's usually followed with something highly offensive."   6

"Make more moves and less announcements."   7

Speak:

"Cultivate the habit of speaking well of others. Dwell upon the good qualities of those with whom you associate, and see as little as possible of their errors and failings. When tempted to complain of what someone has said or done, praise something in that person's life or character. Cultivate thankfulness. Praise God for His wonderful love in giving Christ to die for us."   1

"Don't speak evil of someone if you don't know for certain, and if you do know ask yourself, why am I telling it?"   2

"Me and my best friend can speak to each other through facial expressions."   3

Speak - Miscellaneous:

"It's better to make a difference than to make a point."   4

"The greatest problem in communication is the illusion that it has been accomplished."   5

"Be a good listener. Your ears will never get you in trouble."

6

Speech:

"Self-restraint and gentle speech are effective against stubborn opposition."

1

"Encourage all to use simple, pure, elevated language. Speech, pronunciation, and voice—cultivate these talents, not under any great elocutionist of the world, but under the power of the Holy Spirit of God."

2

Criticism:

"There are two types of criticism, one for correction and one for destruction. Make sure you know the difference."

1

"A critic is a man who knows the way but can't drive the car."

2

"Don't be distracted by criticism. Remember—the only taste of success some people have is when they take a bite out of you."   3

"Whoever stubbornly refuses to accept criticism will suddenly be destroyed beyond recovery."
(Proverbs 29:1)   4

"You can't let praise or criticism get to you. It's a weakness to get caught up in either one."   5

"Whenever you feel like criticizing any one, just remember that all the people in this world haven't had the advantages that you've had."   6

"Do reflect on your own behavior. Don't blame others for criticizing you."   7

"To avoid criticism, do nothing, say nothing, be nothing."   8

Criticism - Miscellaneous:

"Everyone thinks I'm showing off when I talk,
ridiculous when I'm silent, insolent when I answer,
cunning when I have a good idea, lazy when I'm tired,
selfish when I eat one bite more than I should."   9

"People in glass houses shouldn't throw stones"   10

Excuse:

"Never ruin an apology by adding an excuse."   1

"If you are looking for excuses, you will always find
one."   2

"If it is important enough to you, you will find a way. If
it is not, you will find an excuse."   3

"In our own case, we accept excuses too easily; in other
people's, we do not accept them easily enough."   4

Eutrapelia VI

"Hearing aid for sale. Give me a shout if you're interested."

"Light travels faster than sound. That's why some people appear bright until you hear them speak."

"Most sports consists of a few men on a field desperately in need of a rest and 50,000 in the stands desperately in need of exercise."

"Golf isn't just a sport. It's a way of pretending you're getting exercise."

Chapter Seven

Family

———◆◆◆———

Parents:

"Love your parents. We are so busy growing up, we often forget they are also growing old."

1

"By the time I realized my parents were right, I had kids that didn't believe me."

2

"Most of us become parents long before we have stopped being children."

3

"The quickest way for a parent to get a child's attention is to sit down and look comfortable."

4

"The thing that impresses me most about America is the way parents obey their children."   5

Mother:

"'Working mother' is redundant. All mothers work."   1

"But there's a story behind everything. How a picture got on a wall. How a scar got on your face. Sometimes the stories are simple, and sometimes they are hard and heartbreaking. But behind all your stories is always your mother's story, because hers is where yours begin."   2

"Simply having children does not make mothers."   3

"There is only one pretty child in the world, and every mother has it."   4

"Instant availability without continuous presence is probably the best role a mother can play."   5

Father:

"I have noticed that there is nothing more invisible or unknown than the father of the child of the single mother."   1

"It is much easier to become a father than to be one."   2

"The moment when the father of the bride passes the responsibility of headship of the newly formed household is profound, yet mostly uncelebrated. Fathers everywhere should take that precious moment to say a word and pass that mantle with grace."   3

"The greatest thing a father can do to his children, is to love their mother."   4

"Any man can be a father. It takes someone special to be a dad."   5

"Being a great father is like shaving. No matter how good you shaved today, you have to do it again tomorrow."   6

Children:

"The best way to educate children to respect their father and mother is to give them the opportunity of seeing the father offering kindly attentions to the mother, and the mother rendering respect and reverence to the father. It is by beholding love in their parents that children are led to obey the fifth commandment."   1

"Do not handicap your children by making their lives easy."   2

"Each day of our lives we make deposits in the memory banks of our children."   3

"Children are the living messages we send to a time we will not see."   4

"Too often we give children answers to remember rather than problems to solve."   5

"How you speak to your children becomes their inner voice." 6

Friend:

"A friend is someone who is there for you when he'd rather be anywhere else." 1

"Friends are like elevator buttons, they can either take you up or bring you down." 2

"A true friend compliments you publicly and corrects you privately. Who can count on you to do this?" 3

"If you see a friend without a smile; give him one of yours." 4

"Best friends don't necessarily have to talk every day. They don't even need to talk for weeks. But when they do, it's like they never stopped talking." 5

Eutrapelia VII

"If a husband said he'll fix it, he will. There is no need to remind him about it every six month."

"I wear the pants in my family. However, my wife buys the pants, washes and irons them, and tells me which pair to put on."

"You're driving a car. It isn't a telephone booth, a beauty parlor, or a restaurant."

"With his phone broken, he was freed up to do other things, like stare at his phone and wish it weren't broken."

Chapter Eight

Wellness

———◆◆◆———

Health:

"The greatest wealth is health." [1]

"If you have health, you probably will be happy, and if you have health and happiness, you have all the wealth you need, even if it is not all you want." [2]

"Good health is a duty to yourself, to your contemporaries, to your inheritors, to the progress of the world." [3]

"Poor health is not caused by something you don't have; it's caused by disturbing something that you already have. Healthy is not something that you need to get, it's something you have already if you don't disturb it."   4

"My own prescription for health is less paperwork and more running barefoot through the grass."   5

"In a disordered mind, as in a disordered body, soundness of health is impossible."   6

"Preserving the health by too strict a regimen is a wearisome malady."   7

"It's bizarre that the produce manager is more important to my children's health than the pediatrician."   8

"If by gaining knowledge we destroy our health, we labor for a thing that will be useless in our hands."   9

"Health and cheerfulness naturally beget each other."   10

"Health... is not so much a state, but a force: the power to resist and overcome threats to one's well-being."   11

"Health is not valued until sickness comes."   12

Illness:

"The most important thing in illness is never to lose heart."   1

"Illness tells us what we are."   2

Sickness:

"There is something in sickness that breaks down the pride of manhood."   1

"Sickness comes on horseback but departs on foot."   2

"It is a lot harder to keep people well than it is to just get them over a sickness."   3

"To avoid sickness eat less; to prolong life worry less."   4

Disease:

"The appearance of a disease is swift as an arrow; its disappearance slow, like a thread."   1

"An imaginary ailment is worse than a disease."   2

"When it comes to eating right and exercising, there is no 'I'll start tomorrow.' Tomorrow is disease."   3

"Stretching oneself too thin is the disease of modern life—letting oneself get too thick, the other."   4

"Against diseases, here the strongest fence
Is the defensive virtue: abstinence."   5

"The deviation of man from the state in which he was originally placed by nature seems to have proved to him a prolific source of disease."   6

Doctor:

"He who takes medicine and neglects to diet wastes the skill of his doctors."   1

"The patient should be made to understand that he or she must take charge of his own life. Don't take your body to the doctor's office as if it were a repair shop."   2

"A good laugh and a long sleep are the best cures in the doctor's book."   3

"Fresh air impoverishes the doctor."   4

"I think you might dispense with half your doctors if you would only consult Dr. Sun more."   5

Physician:

"The physician who teaches people to sustain their health is the superior physician. The physician who waits to treat people until after their health is lost is considered to be inferior. This is like waiting until one's family is starving to begin to plant seeds in the garden."   1

"Everyone should be his own physician. We ought to assist and not force nature. Eat with moderation what agrees with your constitution. Nothing is good for the body but what we can digest. What medicine can produce digestion? Exercise. What will recruit strength? Sleep. What will alleviate incurable ills? Patience."   2

Drug:

"The longer I live the less confidence I have in drugs and the greater is my confidence in the regulation and administration of diet and regimen."   1

"Half the modern drugs could well be thrown out the window, except that the birds might eat them."   2

Drug - Miscellaneous:

"With every pill we have prescribed for us we should also be given a creative prayer, a suggested way to correct our destructive patterns of thought." 3

"Sometimes I get the feeling the aspirin companies are sponsoring my headaches." 4

Heal:

"To heal is to touch with love that which we previously touched with fear." 1

"Leave your drugs in the chemist's pot if you can heal the patient with food." 2

Food:

"Food is the most abused anxiety drug. Exercise is the most underutilized antidepressant." 1

"During the world changing agricultural market, what we choose to buy today, is what we tell the farmer's to grow tomorrow. Choose your food and you choose your freedom." 2

Food - Miscellaneous:

"Adam and Eve ate the first vitamins, including the package." 3

Remedies:

"There are some remedies worse than the disease." 1

"Our body is a machine for living. It is organized for that, it is its nature. Let life go on in it unhindered and let it defend itself, it will do more than if you paralyze it by encumbering it with remedies." 2

"Pure air, sunlight, abstemiousness, rest, exercise, proper diet, the use of water, trust in Divine power— these are the true remedies." 3

Air:

"Fresh air, exercise, pure water, and clean, sweet premises, are within the reach of all with but little expense; but drugs are expensive, both in the outlay of means and the effect produced upon the system." [1]

"You can't change who you are, but you can change what you have in your head, you can refresh what you're thinking about, you can put some fresh air in your brain." [2]

Sunlight:

"Do not anticipate trouble or worry about what may never happen. Keep in the sunlight." [1]

"As a beam of sunlight sent through a room will at once reveal numberless motes floating in the air of the room, so a ray of Divine love let into the heart will immediately make visible to us a cloud of imperfections of which we were before entirely unaware." [2]

Abstemiousness/Temperance:

"Abstemiousness means temperance. True temperance teaches us to dispense entirely with everything harmful and to use judiciously that which is healthful."   1

"Joy and Temperance and Repose
Slam the door on the doctor's nose."   2

Rest:

"The best of all medicines are rest and fasting."   1

"The stomach is exhausted, and no more needs stimulus or food, than a jaded horse needs the whip! What is needed is rest—complete rest."   2

Rest - Miscellaneous:

"Sleep is the best restorer of the nervous system."   3

Exercise:

"Exercise should be regarded as tribute to the heart."   1

"Those who think they have no time for bodily exercise will sooner or later have to find time for illness."   2

Proper Diet:

"A proper diet is the lifestyle of healthy eating, not a
sporadic enrollment to avoid what is unhealthy."   1

"I've found without question that the best way to lead
others to a more plant-based diet is by example—to
lead with your fork, not your mouth."   2

Water:

"Make of water an all time companion"   1

"Drink eight glasses of water or more everyday day."   2

Trust in Divine power:

"He said, 'If you listen carefully to the Lord your God
and do what is right in his eyes, if you pay attention to
his commands and keep all his decrees, I will not bring
on you any of the diseases   I brought on the Egyptians,
for I am the Lord, who heals you.'"   1

"He said to her, Daughter, your faith has healed you. Go
in peace and be freed from your suffering."   2

Eutrapelia VIII

"To some people, the three basic food groups are Canned, Frozen, and Takeout."

"The bank called him because they noticed some 'highly suspicious' activity on his account. It was for a new gym membership."

"The ice cream said it's best if eaten by next spring but I hate to leave things to the last minute."

"TIP FOR REDUCING WEIGHT: Turn your head to the left and then turn to the right. Repeat exercise when offered something fattening to eat."

Chapter Nine

Syllogism

---◆◆◆---

Syllogism - The building block of reason

"Start where you are, use what you have, do what you can." 1

"I do it because I can, I can because I want to, I want to because you said I couldn't." 2

"Yesterday is a cancelled check; tomorrow is a promissory note; today is the only cash you have so spend it wisely." 3

"People are the only investments that matter; Love is the only currency that counts, and grace is the only motivation that lasts." 4

"God works, we trust. We obey, God rewards. God gives, we become givers."   5

"If you want your life to have impact, focus it. Stop dabbling. Stop trying to do it all."   6

"The past is behind, learn from it. The future is ahead, prepare for it. The present is here, live it for God."   7

"Wisdom is knowing what to do next; skill is knowing how to do it; and virtue is doing it."   8

"Don't stress. Do your best. Forget the rest."   9

"Behind me is infinite power; before me is endless possibility; around me is boundless opportunity."   10

"The best and most beautiful things in life cannot be seen, nor touched, but are felt in the heart."   11

"You have weaknesses, but God has strength. You have sin, but God has grace. You fail, but God remains faithful."   12

"You teach people how to treat you by what you allow, what you stop, and what you reinforce."   13

"Live in the sunshine, swim the sea, drink the wild air."   14

"We gain the most when we give. We learn the most when we teach. We receive the most when we serve."   15

"Linger long at the foot of the cross. Immerse yourself in the curriculum of grace. Be grateful for God's unending mercy."   16

"You are a child of God. You are wonderfully made. You are here for a purpose."   17

"Go to bed early, Drink more water, Exercise daily."   18

"Father, may we be generous today with gentle responses, quick repentances, and copious encouragement."   19

"Having a place to go—is a home. Having someone to love—is a family. Having both—is a blessing."   20

"Don't stress. Do your best. Forget the rest."   21

"Be interesting, be enthusiastic... and don't talk too much."   22

"Choose your life with caution, plan your future with purpose, and frame your life with faith."   23

"Jesus redeems: He heals the past; He clarifies the present; He secures the future."   24

"Time is more valuable than money. You can get more money, but you cannot get more time."   25

"Expect the best. Prepare for the worst. Capitalize on
what comes."   26

"Do justly. Love mercy. Walk humbly."   27

"Accept no other order than that of affinities, no other
chronology than that of the heart, no other schedule
than that of unplanned encounters, the true ones."   28

"Be always at war with your vices, at peace with your
neighbors, and let each new year find you a better
man."   29

"God whispers to us in our pleasures, speaks in our
consciences, but shouts in our pains. It is his
megaphone to arouse a deaf world."   30

Chapter Ten

Ontology

—◆◆◆—

Ontology - The philosophy of existence

"What lies behind us and what lies before us are tiny matters compared to what lies within us."   1

"Do not find your identity in your wounds; find it in the One who was wounded for you."   2

"No one in the entire world can do a better job of being you than you."   3

"Your biggest competitor is the person you want to become."   4

"We cannot become what we need to be by remaining what we are."   5

"If you try to be someone else, you rob God of who He is trying to make you to be."   6

"Would you be friends with yourself? Be the friend you want to have."   7

"Always be a first-rate version of yourself, instead of a second-rate version of somebody else."   8

"You are not an avocado; only enjoyable when fully ready. Start loving yourself now."   9

"The best way to cheer yourself up is to cheer somebody else up."   10

"Best way to stand out in a crowd? Be yourself."   11

"Don't place your happiness in someone else's hands, because once they're gone, so is your happiness."   12

"The things we think about, focus on, and surround ourselves with will shape who we are."   13

"Every man's work, whether it be literature, music, architecture or anything else, is always a portrait of himself."   14

"If you act like you should be the center of all things you will be miserable, for you live in a world that does not share your opinion."   15

"You won't be able to change the world, the church, anything, if you don't change yourself."   16

"Stop giving someone else the job of making you happy."   17

"If you don't like how things are, change them! You're not a tree."   18

"Enjoy when you can, and endure when you must."   19

"If you surrender to the wind, you can ride it."   20

"Face what you think you believe and you will be surprised."   21

"Don't look where you fall, but where you slipped."   22

"An 'unemployed' existence is a worse negation of life than death itself."   23

"It's not my responsibility to be beautiful. I'm not alive for that purpose. My existence is not about how desirable you find me."   24

Chapter Eleven

Chiasmus

Chiasmus - The boomerang of life

"The greatest crimes in the world are not committed by people breaking the rules but by people following the rules." [1]

"A society which permits anything will eventually lose everything." [2]

"Right is right even if no one is doing it; wrong is wrong even if everyone is doing it." [3]

"If you don't stand for what's right, you will be consumed by what's wrong." [4]

"The key is not to prioritize what's on your schedule, but to schedule your priorities." 5

"To be old and wise, you must first be young and stupid." 6

"We tend to be so hungry for much of what matters little, and so satisfied with little of what matters much." 7

"It's not the hours you put in your work that counts, it's the work you put in the hours." 8

"My pain may be the reason for somebody's laugh. But my laugh must never be the reason for somebody's pain." 9

"The worst days of those who enjoy what they do are better than the best days of those who don't." 10

"Purpose always produces passion. On the other hand, passion dissipates when you lack a purpose." 11

"It is better to look ahead and prepare than to look
back and regret."   12

"You are either leaving a mark on the world, or it is
leaving a mark on you."   13

"Sometimes you find yourself in the middle of
nowhere, and sometimes in the middle of nowhere,
you find yourself."   14

"Strong people stand for themselves, but stronger
people stand up for others."   15

"We don't get God's attention because we are good; He
gets our attention because He is good."   16

"I would rather walk with God in the dark than go
alone in the light."   17

"I'd rather be hated for who I am, than loved for who I
am not."   18

"The Gospel must be used to comfort the afflicted and afflict the comfortable."   19

"God isn't chasing us because He can't live without us, but because we can't live without Him."   20

"Be careful how you treat people on the way up. For you shall meet them again on the way back down."   21

"The purpose of life is a life of purpose."   22

Chapter Twelve

Some Great Advice

---◆◆◆---

"Hold everything in your hands lightly, otherwise it hurts when God pries your fingers open."

1

"You better do things God's way or you'll have to repeat your homework."

2

"Love the calling you have, not the one you wish that you had."

3

"When a miracle don't happen for you, you can still be a miracle for someone else."

4

"When everything is coming your way, you're in the
wrong lane."   5

"To communicate for transformation, you must touch
the heart, not merely teach the head."   6

"We are a culture that relies on technology over
community, a society in which spoken and written
words are cheap, easy to come by, and excessive.
Our culture says anything goes; fear of God is almost
unheard of. We are slow to listen, quick to speak, and
quick to become angry."   7

People:

"One day, you'll be just a memory for some people. Do
your best to be a good one."   1

"Gravitate to people who are doing productive and
positive things with their lives."   2

"People generally see what they look for, and hear
what they listen for."   3

"People are lonely because they build walls instead of bridges."

4

Relationship:

"Your network is far more valuable than your net worth. Relationships matter most."

1

"To know when to go away and when to come closer is the key to any lasting relationship."

2

Relationship - Miscellaneous:

"Surround yourself with the precious few who believe in you."

3

"You don't have to attend every argument you're invited to."

4

"We need to start to practicing now how to get along with others."

5

Time:

"Time is our most valuable asset, yet we tend to waste it, kill it, and spend it rather than invest it."   1

"The bad news is that time flies. The good news is that you're the pilot."   2

"It is dangerous to be so busy that you have no time to wait on God."   3

"It is possible that we can get so busy doing work 'for' the Lord that we have no time For the Lord."   4

"Great things take time to grow."   5

"All endings are also beginnings. We just don't know it at the time."   6

Control:

"Times get overwhelming when you begin to try to control the uncontrollable. Let go and let God."   1

"The only thing you sometimes have control over is perspective. You don't have control over your situation. But you have a choice about how you view it."   2

Dream:

"Surround yourself with dream makers, not dream killers."   1

"Follow the trail to your dreams, not the path of others' expectations."   2

"It's difficult to follow your dream. It's a tragedy not to."   3

Study:

"Studying makes you smart. Observing makes you wise. Slow down, look closely, then think about what you've seen."   1

"You learn to speak by speaking, to study by studying, to run by running, to work by working; in just the same way, you learn to love by loving."   2

Talent:

"Talents, resources, wisdom, experiences, and ideas come from God. Be sure to use them for good, not evil."   1

"Your talent is God's gift to you. What you do with it is your gift to God."   2

Economy:

"Economic disaster begins with a philosophy of doing less and wanting more."   1

"Forgiveness is the economy of the heart... forgiveness saves the expense of anger, the cost of hatred, the waste of spirits."   2

Money:

"Money is a useful servant but a useless god. If you don't manage money, it manages you."   1

"The veil of money has never been about how much money you have but about how much money has you."   2

Money - Miscellaneous:

"My riches consist not in the extent of my possessions,
but in the fewness of my wants." 3

"Give me five minutes with a person's checkbook, and I
will tell you where their heart is." 4

"Some people have learned to earn well, but they
haven't learned to live well." 5

"The high cost of living is really the cost of high living.
Greed, not need, gets most people into debt." 6

"Make a budget. Plan before you spend, keep a record
of Expenses. A prudent Man Foreseeth." 7

"The fewer things we want, the wealthier we are." 8

"No one has ever become poor by giving." 9

"Abundance is no more a sign of God's blessing than scarcity is a sign of disobedience; for there are rich fools and hungry saints."

10

"Never confuse your net-worth with your self-worth. Your value isn't based on your valuables."

11

"I don't own anything. I'm only managing the resources that God has blessed me with."

12

Eutrapelia IX

"Laughing at your mistakes can lengthen your life. Laughing at someone else's can shorten it."

"Laughter is an instant vacation."

"People like crowds. The bigger the crowd, the more people show up. Small crowd, hardly anyone shows up."

"Always remember that you are absolutely unique. Just like everyone else."

Chapter Thirteen

Christianism

————————◆◆◆————————

Christian:

"Christians don't tell lies, they just go to church and sing them."

1

"Educated Christians like myself expect God's grace to prefer people of greater natural ability, higher standards of behavior, and superior education in the liberal arts. In fact, God mocks my expectations."

2

"Christians get very angry toward other Christians who sin differently than they do."

3

"Most Christians are satisfied living as common Christians, without an insatiable hunger for the deeper things of God."   4

"Christianity is not about the best people making it up to God; it's about God making it down to the worst people."   5

"Christian freedom is not freedom to do what you like, but freedom from all the things that stop you being the person God wants you to be."   6

"Christian, your right standing with God is possible because He has done what was impossible for you."   7

"The Christian life isn't imitation of Christ but inhabitation by Christ."   8

"I believe in Christianity as I believe that the sun has risen – not only because I see it, but because by it I see everything else."   9

"The issue for Christians is not if we are witnesses; the
issue is what kind of witnesses will we be."   10

"If you want a religion to make you feel really
comfortable, I certainly don't recommend Christianity."   11

"How has your Christianity inconvenienced your life
this past week? Or, is it merely a matter of
convenience?"   12

"Spiritual Christians look upon the world not as a
playground but as a battleground."   13

"Christian brotherhood is not an ideal we must realize;
it is rather a reality created by God in Christ in which
we may participate."   14

"Christians who did most for this world were those
who thought most of the next."   15

"Christianity seems at first to be about morality, rules, guilt, and virtue, yet it leads you out of that, into something beyond."   16

"The essence of the Christian message is not 'Behave!' but "Behold!"   17

Christian - Miscellaneous:

"Life of godliness: Palm branches one day, persecution the next."   18

Legalism:

"Have you noticed that Pharisees tend to beat everybody up with the law but themselves? Double-standard legalism."   1

"Legalism... was a poor religion; so far as it prevailed, it only tended to make me gloomy, stupid, unsociable, and useless."   2

Devil:

"The devil is a better theologian than any of us and is a devil still." [1]

"Two errors about devils: One is to disbelieve in their existence. The other is to believe and to feel an obsessive and unhealthy interest in them." [2]

Church:

"If the church does not identify with the marginalized, it will itself be marginalized. That is God's poetic justice." [1]

"People at healthy churches think "service"; people at unhealthy churches think "serve us."" [2]

"God expects us to measure the church not against tradition, but against the standards and promises of His Word." [3]

"If I'm only concerned about my personal growth and not the growth of Christ's Church, my understanding of growth is immature."   4

"The groups that Jesus attracted—irreligious, poor, outcast, social rejects—are the same groups many churches repel. The groups that Jesus offended the most—the religious and the rich—are the same groups that many churches cater to the most."   5

"This is a day of amalgamation and homogenization. The churches are being fused into a world church, the nations into a world state. We hear of a syncretism of world religion. 'Syncretism' is a dignified word for 'hash.' I never eat hash away from home because I don't know what it is made of, and I don't eat it at home because I do know what it is made of! We are not going to improve the bad eggs of humanity by stirring all kinds of eggs into an omelet. A true pastor must not only feed the flock, he must warn the flock. He must not only be zealous but jealous. (II Corinthians 11:2)."   6

Worship:

"I can safely say, on the authority of all that is revealed in the Word of God, that any man or woman on this earth who is bored and turned off by worship is not ready for heaven."   1

"Worship is no longer worship when it reflects the culture around us more than the Christ within us."   2

"The worship leader in heaven would catch flak on earth. No sitting down, and he keeps repeating the same choruses."   3

"We can no more diminish God's glory by refusing to worship Him than a lunatic can put out the sun by scribbling 'darkness' in his cell."   4

"Go to church once a week and nobody pays attention. Worship God seven days a week and you become strange!"   5

"A church that can't worship must be entertained. And leaders who can't lead the church to worship must provide the entertainment."   6

"A disciple is a worshiper of Jesus continually being changed by Jesus to obey Jesus and teach others to do the same."   7

"What a perfectly good day for being grateful for all things and resentful of none; for being a worshiper, not a whiner."   8

Music:

"Music is God's gift to us for expressing emotion."   1

"Music can lift our mind from the earth, and lift up our spirits to heaven."   2

"Music is the prayer the heart sings."   3

"Music speaks what cannot be expressed, soothes the mind and gives it rest, heals the heart and makes it whole, flows from heaven to the soul." [4]

Singing:

"Christ didn't die for the angels, yet they sing to Him. Don't let the angels out sing you today!" [1]

"Sing lustily and with good courage... Be no more ashamed of your voice now than when you sang the songs of Satan." [2]

"Happy are we if we put into practice what we hear and sing." [3]

Prayer:

"Prayer is the opening of the heart to God as to a friend. Not that it is necessary in order to make known to God what we are, but in order to enable us to receive Him. Prayer does not bring God down to us, but brings us up to Him." [1]

"Prayer is the most important conversation of the day."   2

"Preparation helps reduce anxiety and builds confidence. The best preparation is prayer."   3

"Courage is fear that has said its prayers."   4

"Don't panic; pray. Panic is natural; prayer is super-natural."   5

"Prayer gives way to faith, faith gives way to love, and love gives way to service."   6

"Certain thoughts are prayers. There are moments when, whatever be the attitude of the body, the heart is on its knees."   7

Prayer - Miscellaneous:

"Perhaps our eyes need to be washed by our tears once in a while, so that we can see Life with a clearer view again."   8

"The wound is sin, the medicine is repentance"   9

The Lord's Prayer

"The Lord's Prayer was intended by Jesus to bind His followers closely to the agenda of His whole ministry."   1

"Jesus prayed not that we would be taken out of the world, but that we would be kept from evil."   2

About Prayer

"When God answers a prayer, no matter how big or how small, we need to share it. It's a stewardship issue. If we don't turn the answer to prayer into praise, it may very well turn into pride. Giving testimony is the way we give God all of the glory... but we also need to share it because others need to hear it. If we don't share our testimonies of how God is working in our lives, then others are tempted to think He isn't working at all."   1

"When the Bible says "watch and pray," it doesn't mean "watch and criticize," "watch and gossip" or "watch and judge."   2

"If you do all the talking when you pray, how will you ever hear God's answers?"   3

"If God listened to you like you listen to Him, how often would your prayers be heard?"   4

"Prayer is when you talk to God; meditation is when you listen to God."   5

"It's strange that while praying, we seldom ask for a change of character, but always a change of circumstances."   6

"When you pray, don't give God instructions... just report for duty!"   7

"Does the Bible say, 'Preach without ceasing?' or 'Teach without ceasing?' or 'Sing without ceasing?' No. It says, 'Pray without ceasing.'   8

"Prayer should be the key in the morning and the lock at night."   9

"Prayer should be our first choice and way of life; not practiced only as a last resort or in times of emergency."   10

"Pray as though everything depended on God. Work as though everything depended on you."   11

"A sincere prayer gives you peace, the peace of His Holy Spirit."   12

"When you pray, concentrate."   13

The Power of Prayer

"God changes the hearts of people. Prayer changes the heart of God."   1

"Worry increases pressure; prayer releases peace."   2

"Your prayer on earth activates God's power in heaven."   3

"Prayer develops intimacy with God. Difficulties and hardships develop our motivation and willingness to pray."   4

"It's more effective to pray for someone than to preach at someone."   5

"All of us would be wiser if we would resolve never to put people down, except on our prayer lists."   6

"Prayer lets God do what He does best. Take a pebble and kill a Goliath. Take the common, make it spectacular! Pray and see what He can do."   7

"Today people will cross your path who are hard to like. You can prey on them or pray for them. Try what Jesus said."   8

Plea:

"Lord, if you marked our transgressions, who could stand?"   1

"May I read the meltings of thy heart to me
in the manger of thy birth,
in the garden of thy agony,
in the cross of thy suffering,
in the tomb of thy resurrection,
in the heaven of thy intercession."   2

"Lord, give me firmness without hardness,
steadfastness without dogmatism, love without
weakness."   3

"Jesus, turn our theology into doxology today, our
protests into prayers, our worries into worship and
our fears into faith."   4

"My prayer for you today is not that you will like the
sermon or be wowed by the music, but that you will
have an encounter with God."   5

"Father, help us to focus more on the person in front of
us today than the next thing on our to do list."   6

Eutrapelia X

"I was feeling bold, but then I lost my b."

"Okay, who wants to give me a push on my mood swing?"

"As long as there are tests, there will be prayer in public schools."

"94.5% of all statistics are made up."

Chapter Fourteen

God the Father

———■◆■———

"And I said to the man who stood at the gate of the year: Give me a light that I may tread safely into the unknown. And he replied: Go out into the darkness and put your hand into the hand of God. That shall be to you better than light, and safer than a known way." 1

"When God is all you have, then all you have is all you need." 2

"I do not hold the universe in my hand, in my heart or in my mind. The universe holds me, and my God holds the universe." 3

His Sovereignty:

"The sovereign God wants to be loved for Himself and honored for Himself, but that is only part of what He wants. The other part is that He wants us to know that when we have Him we have everything – we have all the rest."   1

"God is the ultimate source of all power, authority, and everything that exists. Only God can make those claims; therefore, it's God's sovereignty that makes Him superior to all other gods and makes Him, and Him alone, worthy of worship."   2

"God is either God of all or not God at all. Semi-sovereignty is not an option."   3

His Power:

"It is no secret what God can do."   1

"God didn't give us a spirit of cowardice (2 Timothy 1:7). So when I have it - I got it from somewhere else."   2

"God owns it all. God gives it all away freely. We should do the same."   3

"Every setback is a setup for a comeback. God wants to bring you out better than you were before."   4

"Puppet in the hands of fortune or fate? Not you! You are in the hands of a living, loving God."   5

"God restores what's broken, dead, or abandoned. He specializes in new beginnings."   6

"An infinite God can give all of Himself to each of His children."   7

"We are all good at seeing what God did. May we get better at seeing what God is doing."   8

"God creates out of nothing. He does what is still more wonderful: He makes saints out of sinners."   9

"Men conquer to enslave, God conquers to liberate."   10

"We're always relying on God – we always have and we always will. Some of us just admit it sooner than others."   11

"Whatever God calls you to do, He equips you to do as well."   12

"God may not get us out of a situation, but He will give us the strength to get through it."   13

"Our God is one that gives life to the dead and calls things that are not, as though they were."   14

"God has you in the palm of His hand. He knows every need, every struggle and every desire. He has it all figured out. He's a supernatural God."   15

His Presence:

"If in our Friday day pursuits we're far from God's presence, we're not in very good shape to worship Him on Sabbath."   1

"Those who seek God earnestly and desperately shall surely come into the glorious light of His presence."   2

"Trying to be happy without a sense of God's presence is like trying to have a bright day without the sun."   3

His Image:

"We are birthed uniquely and marvelously in the image of God."   1

"God made us in His own image so that His image would be shown."   2

"It shows the infinite glory of God that we are all stamped with His image, and yet we are unique."   3

"God looks on me, not as I am, but as Christ is."   4

His Mercy:

"It's a good thing God's mercies are new every morning, because I need them every morning, afternoon, and evening."   1

"God's extravagant mercy is overwhelming to our finite minds and offensive to our religious hearts."   2

"I believe God foreknew me and I believe God chose me. What's hard to believe is that He foreknew me and still chose me!"   3

"God reserves the right to use those who are wrong. What other choice does He have?"   4

"The purpose of God isn't to save us from hell. The purpose of God is to make us like Christ."   5

"God sends his Son—here lies the only remedy. It's not enough to give man a new philosophy or a better religion. A Man comes to men."   6

"God handed over His perfect, infinitely precious Son to be crucified. Nothing greater has ever happened. Or ever will." 7

"There is a gap between where you are right now and where God wants to take you." 8

His Grace:

"Frustration, complication, and misery are available in abundance, but so is God's grace." 1

"Even having the desire to want to change is evidence of God's grace in your life." 2

"Grace is the glue that fixes our brokenness." 3

"Man is born broken. He lives by mending. The grace of God is glue." 4

"God has enough grace to solve every dilemma you face, wipe every tear that you cry, and answer every question you ask." 5

"Mercy prompted the Samaritan to bandage the wounds of the victim. Grace prompted him to leave payment for the victim's care."   6

"Grace goes beyond mercy. Mercy gave the prodigal son a second chance. Grace threw him a party."   7

"God's grace invites you to change your attitude about yourself and take sides with God against feelings of rejection."   8

"The salvation story of the thief on the cross isn't the 'exception' when it comes to how someone is saved. It's the norm. By grace."   9

"Rejecting grace because of people who abuse grace is like rejecting water because of people who contaminate a reservoir."   10

"Grace is God doing for us what we could never do and what we will never deserve."   11

"Educated Christians like myself expect God's grace to prefer people of greater natural ability, higher standards of behavior, and superior education in the liberal arts. In fact, God mocks my expectations."   12

"To reject the grace of God is a common sin, of which everybody is guilty who sees any righteousness in himself or in his deeds."   13

"Whether or not I choose to avail myself of it, God has promised me all the grace I'll need for whatever happens today."   14

"You simply must not under-estimate sin, and you simply cannot over-estimate grace."   15

"The relationship between grace and obedience is like breathing: inhaling (grace), exhaling (obedience). Keep that order!"   16

"The promise of sufficient grace for today is not a cliché or maxim; it's our only hope, peace, and joy."   17

His Righteousness:

"If you obey one thousand years you're no more accepted than when you first believed; accepted on Christ's righteousness, not yours."   1

"Religion will just make you religious, but Jesus will make you righteous."   2

"Justification isn't based on our ability to do good, but on God's ability to make us good."   3

"We're sons and daughters by birth, not by worth."   4

His Will:

"The hard part about discovering God's will is the realization that I have to discard mine."   1

"Doing God's will is the best and truest satisfaction one can have."   2

"God requires us to love people even when we don't like them." [3]

"We take ourselves way too seriously, but don't take God seriously enough." [4]

"Availability is better than ability for God." [5]

His Timing:

"God is rarely ever early, but He is never late according to His timetable. Relax and believe that your times are in His hands." [1]

"Right now, God is working and you will see what He's doing at just the right time. He may not be early, but He won't be late." [2]

His Word:

(See also Chapter 17: *The Word of God*)

"The Word and the Spirit are the two hands of the Father in the world."   1

"The Word of God well understood and religiously obeyed is the shortest route to spiritual perfection. And we must not select a few favorite passages to the exclusion of others. Nothing less than a whole Bible can make a whole Christian."   2

His Love:

"God's love is not restricted to when you think you've performed well. He loves you even when you make mistakes and fail."   1

"I can't brag about my love for God, because I fail Him daily. But I can brag about His love for me, because it never fails."   2

"God loves you because of who God is, not because of anything you did or didn't do."   3

"There's nothing that can separate you from God's love. His love is based on who He is, not on who you are."   4

"Though our feelings come and go, His love for us
does not."   5

"Know and believe the love that God has to us, and you
are secure; that love is a fortress impregnable to all the
delusions and assaults of Satan."   6

"We sinned for no reason but an incomprehensible
lack of love; He saved us for no reason but an
incomprehensible excess of love."   7

"Nails didn't hold God to a cross. Love did! The sinless
One took on the fate of a sinner so we sinners could
take on the fate of a saint!"   8

"God has paid us the intolerable compliment of loving
us, in the deepest, most tragic, most inexorable sense."   9

"God loves you so utterly and completely that He has
given Himself for you in Jesus Christ, His beloved Son."   10

"Sometimes you may feel that God is hard on you and doesn't love you. The truth is, He loves you too much to leave you the way you are."   11

"Over time, I've come to realize God as the Divine Artist and each person as God's noble work of art."   12

"God is interested in the intricacies of our daily life— not just the emergencies, when we are... in danger."   13

Communion:

"Real security can only be found in that which can never be taken from you – your relationship with God."   1

"God designed the human machine to run on Himself. He Himself is the fuel our spirits were designed to burn."   2

"You thought you were going to be made into a decent little cottage: but He is building a palace. He intends to come and live in it Himself."   3

"Apart from God, every activity is merely a passing whiff of insignificance."   4

"You may forget that you are at every moment totally dependent on God."   5

"The truth is, all of us are depending on God. It's just that some are more aware of this than others."   6

"If you are not as close to God as you used to be, who moved?"   7

"When we lose God, it is not God who is lost."   8

"I'm lost when I'm not where I'm supposed to be – with the Father. I'm lost when I'm not who I'm supposed to be – like the Father."   9

"We shall not injure God by remaining ignorant of Him, but shall deprive ourselves of His friendship."   10

"Don't resist God's affection for you. His hands are outstretched toward you in love, not anger."   11

"Don't disqualify yourself. God has already demonstrated His approval of you."   12

"When God is about to make preeminent use of a person, He puts them in the fire."   13

"God uses pressure to create diamonds. What makes you think you are different?"   14

"There is but one good; that is God. Everything else is good when it looks to Him and bad when it turns from Him."   15

"We can see sin as God sees sin, or we can deny or rename sin and falsify the data."   16

See Exodus 20:1-17

"We want more effective programs; God wants more
effective people." 17

"We can't impact God's character, but we can impact
His reputation." 18

"If we never tremble before the Lord, maybe we have
never heard His voice." 19

"Sometimes God lets you hit rock bottom so that you
will know that He is the Rock at the bottom." 20

"When you come to the bottom, you find God." 21

"I gave in, and admitted that God was God." 22

"It is out of our surrender that God can begin to use us
and bless us." 23

"God doesn't look at outward appearances but looks at hearts. Sometimes the weakest are the strongest, and the strongest are the weakest."   24

"All God's giants have been weak men, who did great things for God because they reckoned on His being with them."   25

"A missionary is God's person doing God's work God's way at God's time in God's power wherever he or she is at that moment."   26

Chapter Fifteen

The Son of God

"Jesus is the only picture of God ever taken. To know
Jesus is to know God." [1]

"The whole story of the world - and how we fit into it -
is most clearly understood through a careful, direct
look at the story of Jesus." [2]

"I am so flawed that Jesus had to die for me, yet I am so
loved and valued that Jesus was glad to die for me." [3]

His Birth:

"Once in our world, a stable had something in it that
was bigger than our whole world." [1]

"The irony was constant. This whole earth is actually Jesus' footstool, but at Bethlehem there was 'no crib for his bed.'"   2

"No silk. No hype. No party. No hoopla. Were it not for the shepherds, there would have been no reception."   3

"Wise men and shepherds came to Bethlehem seeking a new king; the new king came to Bethlehem to seek wise men and shepherds."   4

"He was created of a mother whom He created. He was carried by hands that He formed."   5

His Ministry:

"Jesus taught for only three years, yet no one else has ever had such a global impact. He split history into BC and AD."   1

"Sometimes they crashed parties, sometimes they climbed trees, but Jesus always welcomed people desperate to see him. He still does."   2

"The miracle-worker is greater than the miracle. Which
do you seek the most?"   3

His Crucifixion:

"Most holy joy-producing paradox: Jesus went humbly
to the cross, so we can come boldly to His throne."   1

"In inspiring novels, citizens sacrificially die for their
king. In the Bible, the King sacrificially dies for us.
What a God!"   2

"Jesus died for you, knowing you might never love Him
back. That is true love."   3

"I am so flawed that Jesus had to die for me, yet I am so
loved and valued that Jesus was glad to die for me."   4

His Power:

"Who would have thought that a Lamb could rescue
the souls of men?"   1

"John heard a lion but turned and saw a lamb. That's the thing about Jesus: He rarely looks like we expect."   2

"Religion changes your behavior. Jesus changes your heart."   3

"The criteria for coming to Jesus is weariness. Come overwhelmed with life. Come with your wandering mind. Come messy."   4

"We all wish we had some do-overs. The good news is Jesus cannot only cleanse our temples, He can re-cleanse them!"   5

His Resurrection:

"Jesus Christ didn't rise from the dead so that we could usurp our doctrinal superiority over another brother."   1

"In the presence of God, in defiance of Satan, Jesus Christ rises to your defense. He offers unending intercession on your behalf."   2

The Way:

"When it comes to Jesus being The Way, it's important for us to remember that we're called to promotion of The Way and not management." [1]

"Jesus does not give recipes that show the way to God, as other teachers of religion do. He is himself, the way." [2]

"There are a thousand ways to be broken and only one way to be made whole." [3]

Communion:

"Friends come and go, but Jesus comes and stays." [1]

"The greatest friend we have is Jesus. He alone listens anytime. He alone loves all times." [2]

"It is possible to know all about doctrine and still not know Jesus." [3]

"The closer you get to me, the less impressive I am. The closer you get to Jesus, the more impressive He is."   4

"The closer we are to Jesus, the further we'll be from sin. The Spirit's fruit is caught through proximity, not achieved through effort."   5

"To see our sin and not see Jesus, is despairing. To see Jesus and not see our sin, is delusional."   6

"The One who saved your soul longs to remake your heart. Let's fix our eyes on Jesus. Perhaps in seeing Him, we will see what we can become!"   7

"I love the idea of Jesus being a lamb. It's the whole thing of Him sending me out as one I struggle with."   8

"Being radically committed to comfort and convenience doesn't mesh well with being radically committed to Jesus. Something's got to give."   9

"We do not 'find Jesus.' Jesus is not lost. We are. Jesus finds us, and in this finding, everything changes."   10

"I love that Jesus meets us where we are, not where we ought to be. And I love that He always takes us someplace better."   11

Christ:

"I believe in Christ like I believe in the sun, not because I can see it, but by it I can see everything else."   1

"Previously, I believed it to be arrogance for one to confidently say, 'I am saved;' but now, as I make that claim, I'm boasting in Christ alone!"   2

His Birth:

"Herod now invited the magi to a private interview. A tempest of wrath and fear was raging in his heart, but he preserved a calm exterior, and received the strangers courteously. He inquired at what time the star had appeared, and professed to hail with joy the intimation of the birth of Christ."   1

"How many observe Christ's birthday. How few, His
precepts." 2

His Love:

"Love goes the distance . . . and Christ traveled from
limitless eternity to be confined by time, in order to
become one of us." 1

"He loves you. He has looked at your life and made this
decision. You are worth dying for." 2

His Power:

"When people say "I can do all things through Christ
who strengthens me," their emphasis is too often on "I
can," rather than "through Christ." 1

"There is nothing that you need between here and
heaven which is not provided in Jesus Christ." 2

"Which way is it going to be? My way or Christ's way?" 3

Communion:

"If Christ is removed from your heart, a void is created that all the created universe cannot fill."　1

"The faith of Christ offers no buttons to push for quick service. The new order must wait the Lord's own time, and that is too much for the man in a hurry. He just gives up and becomes interested in something else."　2

"Following Christ cost the early saints everything. What is it costing us?"　3

"It is either all of Christ or none of Christ! I believe we need to preach again a whole Christ to the world – a Christ who does not need our apologies, a Christ who will not be divided, a Christ who will either be Lord of all or will not be Lord at all!"　4

Chapter Sixteen

The Holy Spirit

—◆◆◆—

"Change is essential for growth, but if we're not under leadership of the Holy Spirit, what will we become?" 1

"A life governed by the Holy Spirit's leadership cannot help but grow in love and compassion." 2

"A church without the Holy Spirit is not a church. It's like a carousel going in circles with a few riders, headed nowhere." 3

Holy:

"The more holy a man becomes, the more conscious he is of unholiness." 1

"You can speak with spiritual eloquence, pray in public, and maintain a holy appearance... but it is your behavior that will reveal your true character."   2

The Spirit:

"David had it all - handsome, a poet, warrior, a heart God was looking for. And yet he still needed the anointing of the Spirit of God."   1

"The closer we are to Jesus, the further we'll be from sin. The Spirit's fruit is caught through proximity, not achieved through effort."   2

"Calm people are just self-controlled people. It's a fruit of the Spirit."   3

Spiritual:

"A Pharisee is hard on others and easy on himself, but a spiritual man is easy on others and hard on himself."   1

"Complacency is easy . . . and it is a deadly foe of spiritual growth."   2

"Having true spiritual discernment, rather than pious shoptalk, is about as popular as a skunk at a picnic."   3

"Spiritual maturity isn't measured by how high you jump in praise, but how straight you walk in obedience."   4

"Spiritual maturity is never an end in itself. We grow up in order to give out."   5

The Fruits of the Spirit:

"But the fruit of the Spirit **is _love_, _joy_, _peace_, _longsuffering_, _gentleness_, _goodness_, _faith_, _Meekness_, _temperance_:**[1] against such there is no law."   1

Love:

"In this life we cannot always do great things. But we can do small things with great love."   2

---

[1] The underlined, represent the fruits of the spirit mentioned in the Bible. Some underlined topics are referenced by their quotes, others are followed by its synonym which would be the one referenced instead, by their quotes.

"Love can melt the hardest heart, heal the wounds of the broken heart, and quiet the fears of the anxious heart."   3

"Love is not a feeling we have; it's a decision to treat people the way Jesus would treat them."   4

"You are both an object and an agent of God's amazing love. Don't be a secret agent!"   5

"Most think of 'perfect love' in terms of romance. When Jesus spoke of perfect love it had to do with how we treat our enemies."   6

"Maybe the people who are hardest to love are the ones who need it the most."   7

"Love your parents. We are so busy growing up, we often forget they are also growing old."   8

"Unconditional love doesn't mean unconditional approval. God (and you) can love people without approving of all they do."   9

"Our love is not to be sealed up for special ones. Break the bottle, and the fragrance will fill the house."   10

"Love is a fruit in season at all times, and within reach of every hand."   11

"For all the things done in its name, Love should complain more about identity theft."   12

"It's not our footprints on the sands of time that will be remembered, but our imprints on the hearts of those we love."   13

Love-for others:

"It's not the urge to surpass all others at whatever the cost, but the urge to serve others at whatever cost."   14

"Real living is living for others."   15

Love-for others - Miscellaneous:

"Godly competition = Outdo one another in showing honor." (Rom. 12:10)   16

"Service is the rent we pay for living in this world of ours."   17

"I always wondered why somebody didn't do something about that, then I realized I am somebody."   18

Joy, Happiness:

"One filled with joy preaches without preaching."   1

"The incomplete joys of this world will never satisfy the [human] heart."   2

"Joy is the appropriate attitude in which to help others."   3

Happiness:

"What is true happiness? It's not attained through self-gratification but through fidelity to a worthy purpose."   1

"Contrary to popular belief, the path to happiness and the path to holiness are in fact the same path."   2

Peace:

"Remaining calm in adversity is a sign of great spiritual strength. No matter what's going on in your life right now, "Hold your peace!"   1

"Peace on the outside comes from knowing God on the inside."   2

"Peace is not the absence of affliction, but the presence of God."   3

"When we put our cares in His hands, He puts His peace in our hearts."   4

"There's always something to be upset about. Inner peace is a choice." 5

"God has a perfect timing for everything. Learn to wait on Him. This brings Him honor, and it brings you peace." (see Psalm 27:14) 6

<u>Longsuffering</u>, Patience:

"We could never learn to be brave and patient if there were only joys in the world." 1

"Patience is the companion of wisdom." 2

"In the Bible, the race of life is never considered from the viewpoint of speed. We are to run it with patience." 3

<u>Gentleness</u>, Kindness:

"Kindness is the language which the deaf can hear and the blind can see." 1

"Unkind people need your kindness the most. They advertise their pain."   2

"Be kinder than necessary, because everyone you meet is fighting some sort of battle."   3

Gentleness, Kindness - Miscellaneous:

"Men and women are not perfect, yet God uses them: if they are good enough for Him, why should we refuse to work with them?"   4

"God sees people as His own treasures, so be careful how you treat them."   5

"Jesus treats us far better than we deserve; and as He has treated us, so we are to treat others."   6

Goodness:

"Goodness is easier to recognize than to define."   1

"Goodness is not achieved in a vacuum, but in the company of other men, attended by love"   2

Faith, Trust, Believe:

"Faith is permitting ourselves to be seized by the things we do not see."   1

"Feed your fears and your faith will starve. Feed your faith and your fears will."   2

"Fear and faith are opposites. Which one increases in your heart depends on which one you feed the most."   3

"Your faith is not to help you avoid problems but to go through problems with stability."   4

"The walk of faith is to live according to the revelation we have received, in the midst of the mysteries we can't explain."   5

"Don't know if trials cause us to lose our faith. Instead, they may just reveal that our faith wasn't as deep as we previously thought."   6

"The cable of faith casts out the anchor of hope and lays hold of the steadfast rock of God's promises."   7

"Faith is: Following without knowing where, Waiting without knowing when, Believing without knowing how, Trusting without knowing why."   8

"I have learned that faith means trusting in advance what will only make sense in reverse."   9

Trust:

"I know God will not give me anything I can't handle. I just wish that He didn't trust me so much."   1

"Trust God's hold on you, more than your hold on God."   2

"It is not just trust; it is not just obey. It is trust and obey."

3

"Many things about our salvation are beyond our comprehension, but not beyond our trust."

4

"All that I have seen teaches me to trust God for all I have not seen."

5

"Our future is not tied to making the right decisions but trusting the right Lord."

6

"Jesus is the only one who has it all together. So let's trust and follow Him."

7

"Satan seeks to defeat you by tempting you to trust your own wisdom. Trust in God."

8

"If God was small enough for you to completely understand Him, He wouldn't be big enough for you to completely trust Him."

9

"Sometimes God removes things from our lives for our own protection. Trust in Him."   10

"When God pushes you to the edge, trust Him fully because only two thing can happen. Either He'll catch you when you fall or He will teach you how to fly."   11

"I can trust the One who has my best interest in mind."   12

"When you have doubts and questions, choose to say Lord, 'I believe. I may not always understand, but I trust You.'"   13

"This year, God cannot be trusted to give you everything you want, but you can trust Him completely for everything you need."   14

Believe:

"I believe in loving imperfect people because Jesus did, and because that's the only kind of people there are to love."   1

"It is unbelievable what unbelievers have to believe in order to be unbelievers." 2

"Believe what God believes about you - you did not come from his factory, you came from his heart." 3

Meekness, Humility:

"Humility is not thinking less of yourself, but thinking of yourself less." 1

"It takes humility to seek feedback. It takes wisdom to understand it, analyze it, and appropriately act on it." 2

"To get near humility, even for a moment, is like a drink of cold water to a man in a desert." 3

"Humility is the first, second, and third ingredient of godliness." 4

Meekness, Humility - Miscellaneous:

"The strongest people are not those who show strength in front of us, but those who win battles we know nothing about." [5]

"One man cannot hold another man down in the ditch without remaining down in the ditch with him." [6]

"Humans write books teaching how to 'make it to the top'. Jesus teaches us how to "get to the bottom." [7]

Temperance:

"In order rightly to understand the subject of temperance, we must consider it from a Bible standpoint; and nowhere can we find a more comprehensive and forcible illustration of true temperance and its attendant blessings, than is afforded by the history of the prophet Daniel and his Hebrew associates in the court of Babylon." [1]

"Alexander found it much easier to subdue kingdoms than to rule his own spirit. After conquering nations, this so-called great man fell through the indulgence of appetite,--a victim of intemperance." 2

"In order for the people of God to be in an acceptable state with him, where they can glorify him in their bodies and spirits, which are his, they must with interest and zeal deny the gratification of appetite, and exercise temperance in all things. Then they can comprehend the truth in its beauty and clearness, and carry it out in their lives." 3

Chapter Seventeen

The Word of God

————————————

Bible:

"It is Christ Himself, not the Bible, who is the true word of God. The Bible. . . will bring us to Him." [1]

"God gave the Bible not so we can know it, but so we can know and love God through it." [2]

"Many books can inform you, but the Bible can transform you." [3]

"There is scarcely anything as dull and meaningless as Bible doctrine taught for its own sake." [4]

"The big problem is not whether the Bible is true. The big problem is whether it is true in you."   5

"Even Satan can quote the Bible for his own purpose."   6

"The Bible was written in tears, and to tears it yields its best treasures."   7

"The Bible isn't a script for a funeral service. It is the record of God bringing life where we expected to find death."   8

"The Bible is God's voice speaking to us, just as surely as if we could hear it with our ears. If we realized this, with what awe we would open God's Word, and with what earnestness we would search its precepts."   9

"One reason the Bible is still so relevant today is that we are still struggling with much of the same stuff 2000 years later."   10

"A Bible that's falling apart, usually belongs to
someone who isn't."   11

Bible Characters:

"David had it all - handsome, a poet, warrior, a heart
God was looking for. And yet he still needed the
anointing of the Spirit of God."   1

"King David loved to gaze upon the beauty of God. He is
considered to be the greatest king of Israel. I think he
was on to something."   2

"You will certainly carry out God's purpose, but it
makes a difference to you whether you serve like Judas
or like John."   3

"Being 'highly favored' by God doesn't mean our path
will be always easy. Consider Mary."   4

Scripture:

"The Scriptures may guide those adrift on the sea of
life back into the harbor of the divine will."   1

"Most scriptures speak to us; the Psalms speak for us."   2

Verse:

"When you memorize a verse, you own it. Then when you meditate on it, it owns you!"   1

"Stop listening for a voice and start looking for a verse. He's already spoken."   2

Verses from the Bible:

"These were more noble than those in Thessalonica, in that they received the word with all readiness of mind, and searched the scriptures daily, whether those things were so."   1

"He humbled you, causing you to hunger and then feeding you with manna, which neither you nor your fathers had known, to teach you that man does not live on bread alone but on every word that comes from the mouth of the Lord."   2

The Gospel:

"The Gospel is an announcement, not an argument. You share it, not shove it."

1

"Resist every temptation to put the works cart before the Gospel horse."

2

"Knowing the Gospel is entirely different than living the Gospel."

3

"The message of the Gospel: The Son of God became a man, so that men could become sons of God."

4

"Jesus says in the Gospel that everyone is wrong, everyone is loved, and everyone is called to recognize this and change."

5

"The Gospel is not only the most important message in all of history; it is the only essential message in all of history."

6

"The Gospel is not my promise to 'turn over a new leaf'; it's God's provision to raise me from the dead."   7

"The Gospels were written to invite readers to enter a worldview."   8

"The Gospel destroys all moats around our churches, and replaces them with bridges and welcome mats."   9

"The only safe 'prosperity Gospel' is one in which Jesus is treasured above everything and generosity is the new gold standard."   10

"Like it or not, the message of the Gospel, when it is announced clearly and without apology, is offensive to some people."   11

The Gospel - Miscellaneous:

"Evangelism involves more dialogue than monologue."   12

"I am a nobody trying to tell everybody about somebody who can save anybody."   13

"We are not diplomats but prophets, and our message is not a compromise but an ultimatum."   14

Truth:

"The truth may sometimes hurt, but it will always help."   1

"Truth divorced from life is not truth in its biblical sense, but something else and something less."   2

"I fear we have become too apologetic in our apologetics. In trying to please everyone we end up destroying the truth."   3

"Let's be eager to leave what is familiar for what is true."   4

"It's better to be slapped by the truth than kissed
with a lie."   5

"When a man who has been honestly mistaken learns
truth, he will either quit being mistaken, or quit being
honest."   6

Chapter Eighteen

Promising

——◆◆◆——

Promise:

"God's promises are like the stars; the darker the night the brighter they shine." [1]

"God promises to meet my need, not my greed." [2]

"Herod's rash oath cost John the Baptist his life. Beware of making quick promises." [3]

"When you trust God to fulfill the promises He's given you, all the forces of darkness cannot stop God from bringing your dreams to pass." [4]

"Three great fears in life: rejection, failure, and death. One even greater promise in the face of them: "Fear not, I Am With You."   5

"The promise of satisfaction in worldly loves is an enduring lie that moves the soul to unfaithfulness from its true lover."   6

"When it comes to God's promises, His delays are not His denials."   7

"When God made a promise to Abraham, he swore by himself for he had no one greater to swear by." (Hebrews 6:13)   8

Promise – Miscellaneous:

"Some of our greatest rewards will come from activities we could not measure."   9

"Floodgates are inadequate to hold back all God has in store for you."   10

"God has a blessing with your name on it."   11

"Where God guides, He provides."   12

"Jesus will bring wine to your table, sight to your eyes, strength for your step and, most of all, power over your grave."   13

Hope:

"God spoke through a donkey and used another as His vehicle of choice. Which means there's hope for all of us who act like one."   1

"When your mind says give up, hope whispers one more try."   2

"Don't spend time beating on a wall. hoping to transform it into a door."   3

"Don't lose hope. When you are down to nothing, God is up to something."   4

"My hope isn't in my abilities, intelligence, or character, but the abilities, intelligence and character of the One who made me." 5

"With Christ, endless hope. Without Him, hopeless end." 6

"The vague and tenuous hope that God is too kind to punish the ungodly has become a deadly opiate for the consciences of millions." 7

"Without the cross, man has no union with the father. On it depends our hope. From it shines the light of His love." 8

"Jesus didn't redeem us with the hope we'd get our act together. Jesus redeemed us because we'd never get our act together." 9

"They gave our Master a crown of thorns. Why do we hope for a crown of roses?" 10

"Our hope of salvation, forgiveness, peace in death and joy in the life to come, rests on who God is, not on how we feel."   11

Thankfulness:

"What if you woke up today with only the things you thanked God for yesterday?"   1

"I may not be where I need to be but I thank God I am not where I used to be!"   2

"The worst moment for the atheist is when he is really thankful and has nobody to thank."   3

Thankfulness – Miscellaneous:

"Feeling gratitude and not expressing it is like wrapping a present and not giving it."   4

Heaven:

"Lower your expectations of earth. This isn't heaven, so don't expect it to be."   1

"Aim at heaven and you will get earth thrown in. Aim at earth and you get neither."   2

"The fact that our heart yearns for something earth can't supply is proof that heaven must be our home."   3

"God has been preparing heaven for you. So don't chafe when He does what He must to prepare you for heaven."   4

"Our greatest deliverance in Heaven will be from ourselves—our corruption, our self-righteousness, our hypocrisy."   5

"My soul can find no staircase to heaven unless it be through earth's loveliness."   6

Kingdom:

"Find the door of your heart, and you will discover it is the door to the kingdom of God."   1

"There are no grandchildren in God's kingdom.
Everyone enters through a one-on-one encounter."   2

Kingdom - Miscellaneous:

"The more fascinated we become with the toys of this
world, the more we forget that there's another world
to come."   3

Chapter Nineteen

Yester days

————————

The Past:

"Never focus on the past – It brings tears.
Don't worry about the future – It brings fears.
Live this moment with a smile – It brings cheers." 1

"Forget what hurt you in the past, but never forget
what it taught you." 2

"Your past may be a nice place to visit, but certainly
not to stay." 3

"It's easy to carry the past as a burden instead of a
school. It's easy to let it overwhelm you instead of
educate you." 4

"You're a product of your past but you're not a prisoner of it. You can choose to change."   5

"Do not let the shadows of your past darken the doorstep of your future."   6

"Those who have hurt you in the past can't continue to hurt you now unless you hold on to the pain."   7

"The next time the devil reminds you of your past, remind him of his future."   8

"We all have setbacks in our yesterdays. But your past doesn't define your future. Today is a new day."   9

"Look not mournfully into the past. It comes not back again. Wisely improve the present. It is thine. Go forth to meet the shadowy future, without fear, and with a manly heart."   10

"The past sure has a funny way of not staying in place as it should."   11

"The past is a foreign country; they do things
differently there."   12

"The one charm of the past is that it is the past."   13

"We need not destroy the past. It is gone."   14

"Bring the past only if you are going to build from it." 15

"God has no power over the past except to cover it with
oblivion."   16

The Past - Miscellaneous:

"You can't change what has already happened so
choose to look ahead instead of behind you."   17

"Sometimes, you will never understand the true value
of a moment until it becomes a memory."   18

"Never let those who stole your yesterday rob your tomorrow. Let it go and move on." 19

"You may be grumbling now. But likely years from now, you'll be looking back on today and saying, "Oh for the good old days!" 20

"Linger too long in the stench of your hurt, and you'll smell like the toxin you despise." 21

"Getting over a painful experience is much like crossing monkey bars. You have to let go to move forward." 22

"Let go of the disappointments and setbacks in your life and hang on to the promises of God for your future." 23

"Look not at the days gone by with a forlorn heart. They were simply the dots we can now connect with our present, to help us draw the outline of a beautiful tomorrow." 24

Forgive:

"He who refuses to forgive is thereby casting away his own hope of pardon."   1

"Forgiveness does not mean approval. You aren't endorsing misbehavior."   2

"We are vengeful. God is forgiving. We remember. God redeems."   3

"A reality of forgiveness: We live with consequences of others' sins while choosing not to hold it against them. Just as God does with us."   4

"Forgiveness liberates the soul. It removes fear. That is why it is such a powerful weapon."   5

"Want to learn to forgive? Then consider how you've been forgiven."   6

"They say 'time heals all things,' but if unforgiveness is at work, "time heals no things.""   7

"No one is a stranger here – everyone belongs;
Finding our forgiveness here, we in turn, forgive all
wrongs."   8

"If God forgives us, we must forgive ourselves; otherwise
it's like setting up ourselves as a higher tribunal than
Him."   9

"Be strong today – forgive someone."   10

"Some people forgive and forget, but always make
sure you don't forget that they forgave you and forgot
about it."   11

"If you're still counting how many times you've forgiven
someone, you're not really forgiving them at all, but
simply postponing revenge."   12

"If you can't forgive and forget, pick one."   13

"To truly forgive is to allow the other person to forget."   14

"Forgiveness is the sweetest revenge." 15

"It's far easier to forgive an enemy after you've got even with him." 16

"Once a woman has forgiven her man, she must not reheat his sins for breakfast." 17

Eutrapelia XI

"I work well with others when they leave me alone."

"I try to stay in touch with reality, but lately it won't return my calls."

"A cookie a day keeps sadness away. A whole box of cookies a day brings it back."

"After only one Karate lesson I can break boards with my cast."

Chapter Twenty

On this day

---◆◆◆---

Today:

"Each day emerges from God's drawing room.
Including this one!" 1

"In God's story, ordinary matters. He enters the world
through folks like you and comes on days like today." 2

"When we make a choice today, we are deciding who
we will be tomorrow." 3

"Isn't it funny how day by day nothing changes, but
when you look back everything has?" 4

"Do something now that will make the person you'll be tomorrow proud to have been the person you are today."

5

"Some things you have to do every day. Eating seven apples on Saturday night instead of one a day just isn't going to get the job done."

6

"God is not as interested in your ability today as he is in your availability."

7

"If you figured it all out today, what would be the point of tomorrow? Enjoy the process of being a work in progress."

8

"When you realize everyone you meet today is deeply loved by God, it takes the pressure off of deciding how to treat them."

9

"Focus on today. God meets daily needs daily, not weekly or annually. He'll give you what you need when it's needed."

10

"Don't be overwhelmed by today's obstacles. The same Spirit that raised Jesus from the dead resides in you."   11

"No matter what I face today, two truths will give me courage: 1) Jesus' tomb is not occupied, 2) His throne is!"   12

"The phrase "do not be afraid" is written in the bible 365 times. That's a daily reminder from God to live every day being fearless."   13

"When we are experiencing dark days, or even dark seasons, our enemy wants us to focus on the darkness. He wants us to believe that darkness is our life. But we follow the light! We are children of the light, we are indwelt by the light and the 'darkness cannot overcome the light.' I choose this day to breathe, walk, and rejoice in the light." (1 John 1:5)   14

"We're never more like Jesus than when we die to self-interest and self-glory, and serve others with joy."   15

Please let us know how you like the book; we would love to have you share your thoughts.

Our email address:

1000favquotes@gmail.com

For daily quotes on social media and upcoming promos:

https://www.facebook.com/worthyofnotice

Thank you and God bless you!

—The author.

Indices

Index of Authors
By Chapter and Topics

Great thanks to *"Quote Investigator-Exploring the Origins of Quotations"* and to Barry Popik.

Websites:

http://quoteinvestigator.com

www.barrypopik.com

Chapter *One* - *Living* - Page 17

Life:

Chapter <u>Two</u> - <u>Noetic</u> - Page 25

Mind:

1 - Max Lucado

2 - Martin Luther King, Jr

3 - Jim Rohn

4 - Unknown

5 - Joyce Meyer

6 - joyce Meyer

7 - Joel Osteen

8 - Tertullian

9 - Joel Osteen

10 - Unknown

11 - Charles Stanley

Decision:

1 - Chris Seidman

2 - Rick Warren

3 - Unknown

4 - Joyce Meyer

5 - Scotty Smith

6 - Ralph Waldo

7 - George Bernard Shaw

8 - H. A. Hopf

9 - Jim Rohn

Choice:

1 - Ellen G. White

2 - Pastor Trieber

3 - Pastor Paul Chappell

4 - Rick Warren

5 - Max Lucado

6 - Ellen G White

7 - Carl Jung

8 - Max Lucado

9 - William Wilberforce

Maturity:

1 - Lawana Blackwell

2 - Rick Warren

3 - Rick Warren

Creativity:

1 - Rick Warren

2 - Scott Adams

3 - Jim Collins

4 - Ayn Rand

Chapter _Three_ – _Hardship_ - Page 35

Adversity:

1 - William Arthur Ward

2 - Acts, Chapter 8

Problem:

1 – A. W. Tozer

2 - Unknown

3 - Scott Williams

4 - Neil Vermillion

5 - Neil Vermillion

6 - Landon Saunders

7 - Corrie Ten Boom

8 - Rick Warren

9 - Joyce Meyer

10 - Joel Osteen

11 - Joyce Meyers

12 - Max Lucado

13 - Unknown

Worry:

1 - Corrie ten Boom

2 - Unknown

3 - Unknown

4 - Unknown

5 - Joyce Meyer

6 - Joyce Meyer

7 - Rick Warren

8 - Unknown

9 - Unknown

10 - Andrés du Bouchet

11- Neil Vermillion

12 - James MacDonald

Difficulty:

1 - Joyce Meyer

2 - Joyce Meyer

3 - Unknown

4 - A. W. Tozer

Trial:

1 - Robert J. Morgan

2 - Henry W. Beecher

Trial – Misc.:

3 - Henry Ford

4 - George Herbert

Chapter <u>Four</u>- <u>Endurance</u> - *Page 45*

Opportunity:

1 - Joel Osteen

2 - Eric Hoffer

3 - Shelby Steele

4 - St. John Chrysostom

Will:

1 - Unknown

2 - Bobby Knight

3 - Jim Rohn

4 - C. S. Lewis

5 - Unknown

6 - Robert Anthony

7 - Unknown

8 - Adrian Rogers

9 - C. H. Spurgeon

10 - C. S. Lewis

11 - C. S. Lewis

Confidence:

1 - Unknown

2 - Jan Jansen

3 - Arthur Ashe

Confidence: - Misc.:

4 - Amethyst Snow-Rivers

Goal:

1 - Antoine de Saint-Exupery

2 - Brian Tracy

3 - Unknown

4 - Rick Warren

5 - Jim Rohn

6 - Josh Patrick

7 - Neil Vermillion

8 - Byrd Baggett

Goal - Misc.:

9 - Rick Atchley

10 - Ralph W. Emerson

Plan:

1 - Joyce Meyer

2 - Rick Warren

3 - Unknown

Chapter *Five* - *Leading* - Page 59

Lead:
1 - Byrd Baggett
2 - Unknown
3 - Rick Warren
4 - Brian Tracy
5 - Donald McGannon
6 - Unknown
7 - Brad Lomenick
8 - Unknown
9 - Unknown
10 - Byrd Baggett
11 - Byrd Baggett
12 - Eric Geiger
13 - Ellen Gould White

Lead – Misc.:
14 – Unknown

Vision:
1 - Byrd Baggett
2 - Helen Keller
3 - Unknown
4 - Unknown

Integrity:
1 - Unknown
2 - Rick Warren

Mediocrity:
1 - Unknown
2 - Unknown
3 - A. W. Tozer

Mediocrity – Misc.:
4 - C. S. Lewis
5 - Max Lucado
6 - Helen Keller
7 - Michelangelo

Pride:
1 - C. S. Lewis
2 – Unknown
3 - C. S. Lewis
4 - Rick Warren

Pride – Misc.:

5 - Max L. Forman

6 - Rick Warren

7 - Augustine

8 - Benjamin Whichcote

Fool:

1 - Dale Carnegie

2 - English Proverbs

3 - Unknown

Pessimist - Optimist

1 - Unknown

2 - Eleanor Roosevelt

3 - Bill Vaughn

Chapter Six - Elocution - Page 67

Word:

1 - Unknown

2 - Ephesians 2:4-10

3 - Neal A. Maxwell

4 - Rick Warren

5 - Scotty Smith

6 - Wendell Johnson

7 - Randy Roper

8 – Unknown

9 - Cheyenne Jones

Say:

1 - Proverbs 16:21
   Rick Warren

2 - Jim Rohn

3 - Mark Twain

Say – Misc.:

4 - Rick Warren

5 - Unknown

6 – Unknown

7 – Unknown

Speak:

1 - Ellen G. White

2 - Johann Kaspar Lavater

3 - Unknown

Speak – Misc.:

4 - Andy Stanley

5 - George Bernard Shaw

6 - Frank Tyger

Speech:

1 - See Proverbs 25:15 -
   Unknown

2 - Ellen G. White

Criticism:

1 - Jeremy Foster

2 - Kenneth Tynan

3 - Zig Ziglar

4 - Proverbs 29:1 -
   New Living Translation
   (NLT)

5 - John Wooden

Chapter _Seven_ - _Family_ - *Page 75*

Parents:

1 - Unknown.

2 - Hussein Nishah

3 - Mignon McLaughlin

4 - Lane Olinghouse

5 - Edward, Duke of
    Windsor

Mother:

1 - Jane Sellman.

2 - Mitch Albom.

3 - John A. Shedd

4 - Chinese Proverb

5 - Lotte Bailyn

Father:

1 - Victor Arias Jr.

2 - Kent Nerburn

3 - Gennarino Brian
    DeStefano

4 - Unknown

5 - Unknown

6 - Reed Markham

Children:

1 - Ellen G. White

2 - Robert A. Heinlein

3 - Charles R. Swindoll

4 - John W. Whitehead

5 - Roger Lewin

6 – Unknown

Friend:

1 - Len Wein

2 - Sheri Rose Shepherd

3 – Rick Warren

4 - Popular Proverb

5 - Unknown

Chapter *Eight* - *Wellness* - *Page 81*

Drug - Misc.:

3 – Ernest Holmes

4 – Terri Guillemets

Heal:

1 - Stephen Levine

2 - Hippocrates

Food:

1 - Unknown

2 - Unknown

Food - Misc.:

3 - E. R. Squibb

Remedies:

1 - Publilius Syrus

2 - Leo Tolstoy

3 - Ellen G. White

Air:

1 - Ellen G. White

2 - Ernesto Bertarelli

Sunlight:

1 - Benjamin Franklin

2 - B. Wilkinson

Abstemiousness/ Temperance:

1 - Unknown

2 - Henry Wadsworth Longfellow

Rest:

1 - Benjamin Franklin

2 - Dio Lewis, M.D.

Rest - Miscellaneous:

3 – The Letter Box – 1859 - Volumes 1-2

Exercise:

1 - Gene Tunney

2 - Edward Stanley

Proper Diet:

1 - Victor Arias Jr.

2 - Bernie Wilke

Water:

1 - Victor Arias Jr.

2 - Unknown.

Trust in Divine Power:

1 - Exodus 15:26
New International
Version (NIV)

2 - Mark 5:34
New International
Version (NIV)

Chapter *Nine* - *Syllogism* - *Page 93*

1 - Arthur Ashe

2 - Unknown

3 - Kay Lyons

4 - Rick Atchley

5 - Neil Vermillion

6 - Rick Warren

7 - Thomas S. Monson

8 - David Starr Jordan

9 - Unknown

10 - Stella Stewart

11 - Helen Keller

12 - Unknown

13 - Tony Gaskins

14 - Ralph Waldo Emerson

15 - Rick Warren

16 - Max Lucado

17 – Rick Warren

18 - Victor Arias Jr.

19 - Scotty Smith

20 - Donna Hedges

21 – Unknown

22 - Norman Vincent Peale

23 - Thomas S. Monson

24 - Parke Brown

25 - Jim Rohn

26 - Zig Ziglar

27 – Micah

28 - Julio Cortázar

29 - Benjamín Franklin

30.- C. S. Lewis

Chapter Ten - Ontology - Page 99

1 - Ralph Waldo Emerson

2 - Rick Atchley

3 - Unknown

4 - Unknown

5 - Max DePree

6 - Miles McPherson

7 - Unknown

8 - Judy Garland

9 - Rita Maria

10 - Mark Twain

11 - Byrd Baggett

12 - Unknown

13 - Unknown

14 - Samuel Butler

15 - Rick Atchley

16 - Tim Keller

17 - Joyce Meyer

18 - Jim Rohn

19 - Johann Wolfgang von Goethe

20 - Toni Morrison

21 - William Hale White

22 - African Proverb

23 - José Ortega y Gasset

24 - Warsan Shire

Chapter Eleven - Chiasmus - Page 103

1 - Banksy

2 - Neal A. Maxwell

3 - Saint Augustine

4 - Byrd Baggett

5 - Stephen R. Covey

6 - Roy Rolfe Gilson

7 - Rick Atchley

8 - Sam Ewing

9 - Charles Chaplin

10 - Jim Rohn

11 - Rick Warren

12 - Jackie Joyner-Kersee

13 - Rick Warren

14 - Unknown

15 - Unknown

16 - Rick Atchley

17 - Mary Gardiner Brainard

18 - Kurt Cobain

19 - Tim Keller

20 - Rick Atchley

21 - Walter Winchell

22 - Robert Byrne

Chapter Twelve - Some Great Advice - Page 107

1 - Corrie ten Boom

2 - Unknown

3 - Jud Wilhite

4 - Nick Vujicic

5 - Steven Wright

6 - Rick Warren

7 - Francis Chan

People:

1 - Unknown

2 - Nadia Comaneci

3 - Harper Lee

4 - Joseph Fort Newton

Relationship:

1 - Rick Warren.

2 - Domenico Cieri Estrada

Relationship – Misc.:

3 - Byrd Baggett

4 - Unknown

5 - Unknown

Time:

1 - Jim Rohn

2 - Michael Altschuler

3 - A. W. Tozer

4 - A. W. Tozer

5 - Byrd Baggett

6 - Mitch Albom

Control:

1 - Unknown

2 - Chris Pine

Dream:

1 - Byrd Baggett

2 - Byrd Baggett

3 - Unknown

Study:

1 - Rick Warren

2 - Anatole France

Talent:

1 – Unknown
   Ecclesiastes 2:26

2 - Leo Buscaglia

Economy:

1 - Jim Rohn

2 - Hannah Moore

Money:

1 - Rick Warren

2 - A. W. Tozer

Money - Misc.:

3 - Joseph Brotherton

4 - Billy Graham

5 - Jim Rohn

6 - Rick Warren

7 - Solomon

8 - Rick Warren

9 - Anne Frank

10 - Scotty Smith

11 - Rick Warren
    See Luke 12:15

12 - Dave Ramsey

Chapter *Thirteen* - *Christianism* - *Page 117*

Christian:

1 - A. W. Tozer

2 - Augustine of Hippo

3 - Philip Yancey

4 - A. W. Tozer

5 - Tullian Tchividjian

6 - Unknown

7 - Unknown

8 - Rick Warren

9 - C. S. Lewis

10 - Rick Atchley

11 - C. S. Lewis

12 - A. W. Tozer

13 - A. W. Tozer

14 - Dietrich Bonhoeffer

15 - C. S. Lewis

16 - C. S. Lewis

17 - Jared Wilson

Christian – Misc.:

18 - John Piper

Legalism:

1 - Scotty Smith

2 - John Newton

Devil:

1 – A. W. Tozer

2 - C. S. Lewis

Church:

1 - Tim Keller

2 - Rick Atchley

3 - A. W. Tozer

4 - Rick Warren

5 - Josh Patrick

6 - Vance Havner

Worship:

1 - A. W. Tozer

2 - A. W. Tozer

3 - Rick Atchley

4 - C. S. Lewis

5 - A. W. Tozer

6 - A. W. Tozer

7 - Jeff Vanderstelt

8 - Scotty Smith

Music:

1 - Rick Warren

2 - John Chrysostom

3 - Unknown

4 - Angela Monet
   Unknown

Singing:

1 - Unknown

2 - John Wesley

3 - Augustine

Prayer:

1 - Ellen G white

2 - Unknown

3 - Unknown

4 - Dorothy Bernard

5 - Neil Vermillion

6 - Unknown

7 - Victor Hugo

Prayer – Misc.:

8 - Alex Tan

9 - St. John Chrysostom

The Lord's Prayer:

1 - N. T. Wright

2 - Neil Vermillion

About Prayer:

1 - Mark Batterson

2 - Joyce Meyer

3 - A. W. Tozer

4 - Lisa Burgess

5 - Diana Robinson

6 - Unknown

7 - Unknown

8 - Max Lucado

9 - Owen Felltham

10 - Rick Warren

11 - Saint Augustine.

12 - Victor Arias Jr.

13 - Victor Arias Jr.

The Power of Prayer:

1 - Unknown

2 - Unknown

3 - Max Lucado

4 – Neil Vermillion

5 - Neil Vermillion

6 - D.A. Carson

7 – Max Lucado

8 - Rick Atchley

Plea:

Chapter _Fourteen_ - _God the Father_ - Page 133

1 - Minnie Louise Haskins

2 - Max Lucado

3 - Unknown

His Sovereignty:

1- A. W Tozer

2 - Chip Ingram

3 - Max Lucado

His Power:

1 - Stuart Hamblen

2 - Chris Seidman

3 - Neil Vermillion

4 - Joel Osteen

5 - Max Lucado

6 - Unknown

7 - A. W. Tozer

8 - Rick Atchley

9 - Soren Aabye Kierkegaard

10 - Burk Parsons

11 - Unknown

12 - Unknown

13 - Joyce Meyer

14 - Romans 4:17 (21st Century King James Version-KJ21)

15 - Joel Osteen

His Presence:

1 - A. W Tozer

2 - A. W Tozer

3 - A. W Tozer

His Image:

1 - Unknown

2 - John Piper

3 - Lois Tverberg

4 - C. H. Spurgeon

His Mercy:

1 - Scotty Smith.

2 - Neil Vermillion

3 - Rick Atchley

4 - Unknown

5 - A. W. Tozer

6 - Dietrich Bonhoeffer

7 - John Piper

8 - Priscilla Shirer

His Grace:

1 - Joyce Meyer

2 - Neil Vermillion

3 - Rick Warren

4 - Eugene O'Neill

5 - Max Lucado

6 - Max Lucado

7 - Max Lucado

8 - Max Lucado

9 - Chris Seidman

10 - Scotty Ward Smith

11- Joyce Meyer

12 - Saint Augustine

13 - Martin Luther

14 - Scotty Ward Smith

15 - Paul David Tripp

16 - Scotty Smith

17 - Scotty Smith

His Righteousness:

1 - Paul David Tripp

2 - Unknown

3 - Rick Warren

4 - Judah Smith

His Will:

1 - Rick Atchley

2 - Victor Arias Jr.

3 - Joyce Meyer

4 - Rick Warren

5 - Unknown

His Timing:

1- Joyce Meyer

2 - Joyce Meyer

His Word:

1 - St. Irenaeus

2 - A. W. Tozer

His Love:

1 - Jonathan Boles

2 - Unknown

3 - Regina Brett

4 - Neil Vermillion

5 - C. S. Lewis

6 - Ellen G. White

7 - Peter Kreeft

8 - Max Lucado

9 - C. S. Lewis

10 - T. F. Torrence

11 - Unknown

12 - Neil Vermillion

13 - A. W. Tozer

Communion:

1 - Rick Warren

2 - C. S. Lewis

3 - C. S. Lewis

4 - Alfred Whitehead

5 - C. S. Lewis

6 - Neil Vermillion

7 - Unknown

8 - Unknown

9 - Chris Seidman

10 - Justin Martyr

11- Neil Vermillion

12 - Neil Vermillion

13 - George MacDonald

14 - Neil Vermillion

15 - C. S. Lewis

16 - A. W. Tozer

17 - Rick Warren

18 - Chris Seidman

19 - Unknown

20 - Tony Evans

21 - Neville Talbot

22 - C. S. Lewis

23 - A. W. Tozer

24 - Neil Vermillion

25 - J. Hudson Taylor

26 - Rick Warren

Chapter Fifteen - The Son of God - Page 151

Jesus:

1 - Max Lucado

2 - Timothy Keller

3 - Augustine of Hippo

His Birth:

1 - C. S. Lewis

2 - Neal A. Maxwell

3 - Max Lucado

4 - Rick Atchley

5 - Augustine of Hippo

His Ministry:

1 - Rick Warren

2 - Rick Atchley

3 - Rick Atchley

His Crucifixion:

1 - Scotty Smith

2 - Rick Warren

3 - Unknown

4 - Timothy Keller

His Power:

1 - Dawn Rodgers and Eric Wyse

2 - Rick Atchley

3 - Dave Stone

4 - Paul E. Miller

5 - Rick Atchley

His Resurrection:

1 – A. W. Tozer

2 - Max Lucado

The Way:

1 - Chris Seidman

2 - Karl Barth

3 - Joe Coffey

Communion:

1 - Unknown

2 - Author Unknowm

3 – Oswald Chambers

4 – Patrick A. Mead

5 – Scott Sauls

6 - Scotty Smith

7 - Max Lucado

8 - Rick Atchley

9 - Chris Seidman

10 - Mike Glenn

11 - Josh Patrick

Christ:

1 - C. S. Lewis

2 - Unknown

His Love:

1 - Max Lucado

2 - Max Lucado

His Birth:

1 - Ellen G. White

2 - Benjamin Franklin

His Power:

1 - Burk Parsons

2 – Charles Spurgeon

3 - A. W. Tozer

Communion:

1 - John Piper

2 - A. W. Tozer

3 - A. W. Tozer

4 - A. W. Tozer

Chapter *Sixteen* - *The Holy Spirit* - *Page 161*

Joy, Happiness:

1 - Mother Teresa

2 - Alexis de Toqueville

3 - St. John Chrysostom

Happiness:

4 - Helen Keller

5 - Josh Patrick

Peace:

1 - Kemmy Nola

2 - Unknown

3 - Unknown

4 - Unknown

5 - Rick Warren

6 - See Psalm 27:14 -
   Joyce Mayer

Longsuffering – Patience:

1 - Hellen Keller

2 - Saint Augustine

3 - A. W. Tozer

Gentleness – Kindness:

1 - Mark Twain

2 - Rick Warren

3 - John Watson

Gentleness - Kindness – Misc.:

4 - Charles Spurgeon

5 - Unknown

6 - Ellen G. White

Goodness:

1 - Wystan Hugh Auden

2 - Saul Bellow
   Dangling Man

Faith, Trust, Believe:

1 - Martin Luther

2 - Max Lucado

3 - Neil Vermillion

4 - Unknown

5 - Bill Johnson

6 - Chris Seidman

7 - David Murray

8 - Unknown

9 - Philip Yancey

Trust:

1 - Mother Teresa

2 - Max Lucado

3 - A. W. Tozer

4 - A. W. Tozer

Chapter *Seventeen* - *The Word of God* - *Page 177*

Bible:

1 - C. S. Lewis

2 - Scott McKnight

3 - Unknown

4 - A. W. Tozer

5 - A. W. Tozer

6 - Rick Warren

7 - A. W. Tozer

8 - Eugene Peterson

9 - Ellen G. White

10 - Chris Seidman

11 - Charles Spurgeon

Bible Characters:

1 - Chis Seidman

2 - Unknown

3 - C. S Lewis

4 - Chris Seidman

Scripture:

1 - St. Gregory of Nyssa

2 - St. Athanasius

Verse:

1 - Buddy Owens

2 - Rick Warren

Verses from the Bible:

1 – Acts 17:11
   King James Bible

2 - Deuteronomy 8:3
   New International Version

The Gospel:

1 - Rick Warren

2 - Scotty Smith

3 - Unknown

4 - Neil Vermillion

5 - Tim Keller

6 - Jerry Bridges

7 - Scotty Smith

8 - N. T. Wright

9 - Scotty Smith

10 - Scotty Smith

11 - Josh Patrick

Chapter *Eighteen* - *Promising* - Page 185

Promise:

1 - David Nicholas

2 - Rick Warren

3 - John Piper

4 - Unknown

5 - Chris Seidman

6 - St. Augustine

7 - Larry Eims

8 - Hebrews 6:13
   King James Version (KJV)

Promise – Misc.:

9 - Unknown

10 - Neil Vermillion

11 - Unknown

12 - Unknown

13 - Max Lucado

Hope:

1 - Chris Seidman

2 - Unknown

3 - Coco Chanel

4 - Unknown

5 - Unknown

6 - Rick Warren

7 - A.W. Tozer

8 - Ellen G. White

9 - Scotty Smith

10 - Martin Luther

11 - A.W. Tozer

Thankfulness:

1 - Unknown

2 - Joyce Meyers

3 - Dante Rossetti

Thankfulness – Misc.:

4 - William Arthur Ward

Heaven:

1 - Max Lucado

2 - C. S. Lewis

3 - C. S. Lewis

4 - Rick Atchley

5 - Randy Alcorn

6 - Michelangelo

Kingdom:

Kingdom – Misc.:

Chapter <u>Nineteen</u> - <u>Yester Days</u> - Page 193

The Past:

1 - Unknown

2 - Unknown

3 - Unknown

4 - Jim Rohn

5 - Rick Warren

6 - Unknown

7 - Mark Lehman

8 - Unknown

9 - Unknown

10 - Henry Wadsworth Longfellow

11 - Unknown

12 - Lesley P. Hartley, *the Go-Between, 1953*

13 - Oscar Wilde, *The Picture of Dorian Gray*

14 - John Cage

15 - Doménico Cieri Estrada

16 - Pliny the Elder

The Past – Misc.:

17 - Unknown

18 - Unknown

19 - Rick Warren

20 - Chuck Swindoll

21 - Max Lucado

22 - C. S. Lewis

23 - Joel Osteen

24 - Dodinsky

Forgive:

1 - Ellen G. White

2 - Max Lucado

3 - A. W. Tozer

4 - Chris Seidman

5 - Nelson Mandela

6 - Max Lucado

7 - Neil Vermillion

8 - Bryan J. Leech

9 - C. S. Lewis

10 - Unknown

11 - Unknown

12 - N. T. Wright

13 - Robert Brault

14 - Robert Brault

15 - Isaac Friedmann

16 - Olin Miller

17 - Marlene Dietrich

Chapter _Twenty_ - _On This Day_ - _Page 201_

Today:

1 - Max Lucado

2 - Max Lucado

3 - A. W. Tozer

4 - C. S. Lewis

5 - Ritu Ghatourey

6 - Jim Rohn

7 - Unknown

8 - Unknown

9 - Rick Atchley

10 - Max Lucado

11 - Neil Vermillion

12 - Rick Atchley

13 - Unknown

14 - Unknown

15 - Scotty Smith

Alphabetical Index of Authors

Alphabetical Index of Authors

50 - Charles Stanley
51 - Cheyenne Jones
52 - Chinese Proverb
53 - Chip Ingram
54 - Chis Seidman
55 - Chris Pine
56 - Chu Hui Weng
57 - Chuck Swindoll
58 - Cicero
59 - Coco Chanel
60 - Corrie ten Boom
61 - D. A. Carson
62 - Dalai Lama
63 - Dale Carnegie
64 - Danish Proverb
65 - Dante Rossetti
66 - Dave Ramsey
67 - Dave Stone
68 - David Murray
69 - David Nicholas
70 - David Starr Jordan
71 - Dawn Rodgers and
     Eric Wyse
72 - Dean Ornish
73 - DeForest Clinton
     Jarvis
74 - Diana Robinson
75 - Dietrich Bonhoeffer
76 - Dio Lewis

77 - Dodinsky
78 - Dolly Parton
79 - Domenico Cieri Estrada
80 - Donald McGannon
81 - Donna Hedges
82 - Dorothy Bernard
83 - Dr Wil Rose
84 - Dutch Proverb
85 - E. R. Squibb
86 - Eduardo Vásquez
87 - Edward Jenner
88 - Edward Stanley
89 - Edward, Duke of
     Windsor.
90 - Edwin Hubbell Chapin
91 - Elbert Hubbard
92 - Eleanor Roosevelt
93 - Ella Wheeler Wilcox
94 - Ellen Gould Harmon
     White
95 - English Proverbs
96 - Eric Geiger
97 - Eric Hoffer
98 - Ernest Holmes,
99 - Ernesto Bertarelli
100 - Eugene O'Neill
101 - Eugene Peterson
102 - F. Scott Fitzgerald
103 - Francis Chan

Index of Topics by Chapter

INDEX OF TOPICS BY CHAPTER

Topics are:

Referenced

Miscellaneous

Topic related

Chapter related

From the Bible

Chapter <u>One</u> - <u>Living</u> - Page 17
1 – Life

Chapter <u>Two</u> - <u>Noetic</u> - Page 25

1 – Mind

2 – Decision

3 – Choice

4 – Maturity

5 – Creativity

6 – Freedom

7 – Liberty

8 – Ignorance

9 – Judge

Chapter <u>Three</u> - <u>Hardship</u> - Page 35

1 – Adversity

2 – Problem

3 – Worry

4 – Difficulty

5 - Trial

6 – Trial

7 – Struggle

8 – Suffering

9 - Failure

10 – Failure

Chapter Nine - Syllogism - Page 93

No Topics

Chapter *Fifteen* - *The Son of God* - *Page 151*

1 – **His Birth**

2 – **His Ministry**

3 – **His Crucifixion**

4 – **His Power**

5 – **His Resurrection**

6 – **The Way**

7 – **Communion**

8 – **Christ**

9 – **His Birth**

10 – **His Love**

11 – **His Power**

12 – **Communion**

Chapter *Sixteen* - *The Holy Spirit* - *Page 161*

1 – **Holy**

2 – **The Spirit**

3 – **Spiritual**

4 – **The Fruits of the Spirit**

5 – **Love**

6 – **Love for others**

7 – **Love-for others**

8 – **Joy**

9 – **Happiness**

10 – **Peace**

Alphabetical Index of Topics

Alphabetical Index of Topics

Topics are:

Referenced

Miscellaneous

Topic related

Chapter related

From the Bible

Eutrapelia.
Index of Authors by
Chapter and sections

Eutrapelia

Eutrapelia:

The adjectival form of this word describes something that turns easily. When applied to intellect it suggests a mental agility and suppleness which can be positive (ready wit) or negative (mockery).

Eutrapelia describes a quickness of wit that was greatly prized in antiquity. It can be used virtuously or wickedly.

Source:

"How Witty Should Christians Be?" by Dr. Larry Perkins.

http://moments.nbseminary.com/archives/how-witty-should-christians-be/

Index notes:

—The number of sections is not the same as the number of chapters.

—Links are provided for informational purposes only and do not constitute endorsement of any products or services provided by these websites. Links are subject to change, expire, or be redirected without any notice.

Chapter One - I - Page 24

1 - Dave Stone

2 - Unknown

3 - Will Rogers

4 - Rick Warren

Chapter Two - II - Page 33

1 - The Fuchsia Fan, (National Fuchsia Society) Volumes 46-48. 1986-88. Page 54

2 - Unknown

3 - Safian 1967: 13

4 - Unknown

Chapter Three - III - Page 43

1 – Unknown

2 – Unknown

3 – Unknown

4 – Unknown

Chapter Four - IV - Page 57

1 - Unknown

2 - Samuel Goldwyn

3 - Unknown

4 - Unknown

Chapter Twelve - IX - Page 115

1 - Unknown

2 - Unknown

3 - Unknown

4 - Unknown

Chapter Thirteen - X - Page 132

1 - Unknown

2 - Unknown

3 - Unknown

4 - Woody Allen

Chapter Nineteen - XI - Page 200

1 - Unknown

2 - Unknown

3 - Unknown

4 - Unknown

1,000 favorite quotes
Much Wisdom in short sayings
by Victor Arias Jr.